PENSIONS LAW HANDBOOK 1999

Eversheds Pensions Law Team

[redacted]

PENSIONS LAW HANDBOOK 1999

Eversheds Pensions Law Team

ISBN 1 90255 814 6

Produced for Eversheds by Palladian, PO Box 15, Bembridge, Isle of Wight PO35 5NQ

Typeset by Adrian McLaughlin

Printed in Great Britain by WBC Book Manufacturers Ltd

Preface

This is the first of what is intended to be an annual Handbook, for the use of scheme managers, actuaries, accountants, trustees and administrators who have cause to become involved with pensions law as part of their work. It is not intended for use by lawyers! The style is mostly short "noddy" guides to subjects of current or continuing interest; each year longer articles, dealing with matters of immediate concern, are included.

The content is written as a joint effort by the Pensions Law Team at Eversheds; some of the longer articles are signed. Suggestions for improvement, ideas for coverage, or any other feedback are always welcome, and developments are already in hand for a more comprehensive volume next year.

If you would like access to our regular newsletters or technical bulletins on pensions law, or a copy of next year's edition, please fill in the form at the back of the book, and we'll make sure you're on the mailing list.

Foreword

Many employers now provide pensions for their employees and some have done so for many years. Indeed it may not be long before such provision is compulsory as the role of the state in the provision of pensions diminishes. The importance of private pension arrangements in the financial affairs of citizens will inevitably increase, especially as the population ages.

It is hardly surprising then that the law takes an increasing interest in pensions matters. It does so to protect the interests of all the people involved in the schemes: the members, the employers, the providers and others. And because pension rights and expectations are so important, there are now more disputes about them.

Unfortunately, the law on pensions is complicated (there are now several thousand pages of pensions legislation) and the deeds and rules governing them are usually long and are sometimes difficult to interpret. Decisions of the courts and the Pensions Ombudsman emerge almost daily and add to the sheer volume of the law.

So anything can help reduce the occasions for, and accordingly the number of, such disputes and improve the understanding of the law relating to pensions and the implications for employers, scheme mangers and other professionals is to be welcomed. This initiative by the Eversheds Pensions Law Team led by Mr Robin Ellison (an acknowledged authority in this field) will serve as a useful and practical guide to pensions law for non-lawyers.

This work, written in a straightforward style and jargon free, covers a wide range of topics and is sure to develop into a standard text which every scheme manager will wish to have to hand to refresh himself or herself on any current legal problem, or to find an appropriate source for further research. I wish it well.

Sir Gavin Lightman

Contents

Thinkpiece

The Euro, inflation, annuities and the real cost of pensions

The pensions conundrum is much the same as the global warming question: is the environment really changing? and if so, is that change permanent? (what is sometimes called a paradigm shift). Or are we seeing no more than a minor swing, perhaps only a tremor, in the pendulum? Change always means that there will be winners and losers. Those who identify the direction and extent of change, and can seize its timing, will be repositioning themselves for maximum advantage. The passive are more likely to suffer.

When we look backwards, further back than the last year or so, most of us can persuade ourselves that as far as the eye can see or the mind remember we have been living with valuation rates of interest of the order of 10 percent, sometimes more and sometimes less, but averaging around that figure over any run of years; and rates of earnings growth which have fluctuated similarly, but averaged around 8 percent. The employer who funded his occupational scheme on those assumptions might have concluded that he could set his contribution rates at:

3.75% for employees aged 25 to 34

7.50% for employees aged 35 to 44

14.25% for employees aged 45 to 54

26.25% for employees aged 55 to 64.

It is not difficult to calculate that 10 years' contributions at 3.75 percent would grow into a fund which — 30 years later, normal retirement age for the employee concerned — would give him a 10/60ths pension based on a notional final salary which had escalated at 5 percent through those same 30 years. If that employee stayed for 20 years rather than 10, the 20 years' contributions would give him a deferred pension of 20/60ths based on his leaving salary escalated at 5 percent for 20 years.

Those calculations require, of course, that one makes certain assumptions about the shape of the annuity that our employer thought he should be providing. He might have estimated, for instance, that a male employee would live for 14 years after retirement, and that his widow would survive him on a half pension for a further six years. His hindsight might have indicated that inflation would inevitably continue unabated throughout the annuity period, but it would also have told him that it was unrealistic for any employer (other than government) to offer full protection to all pensioners – discretionary increases averaging 2.5 percent would be an acceptable norm. And finally, the employer would have assumed that there would be growth in the annuity fund itself, that it would be invested in gilts yielding, say, 9 percent.

All these figures, in both of the last two paragraphs, would have been consistent with occupational schemes' experiences in economic terms over a quarter century from the late 1960s; and all are also consistent actuarially.

An individual providing his own pension on a money purchase basis, assuming that his earnings profile was similar and that he wanted the same annuity, could have paid more or less the same contributions; if there is a factor which differentiates his case it is that a non-negligible amount, of both contributions and annuity fund, could be expected to have leaked away to meet the charges levied by his pension provider.

But those figures all represent the past. What does the forward looking employer, or individual, see today, as he tries to look out into the great unknown? All political parties, not just in the United Kingdom but across Europe, are determined that inflation is the great evil; that it must be squeezed out, or at least down, whatever the cost. Pensions in payment may have to be increased, but the level of the inflation to be taken into account may be of the order of 2.5 or 3 percent.

However, there is a more significant pensions effect of a low inflation rate. The rate at which an early leaver's salary had to be escalated between leaving date and normal retirement age was, when the legislation was introduced, written into section 52B of SSPA 1975, and Sched 1A to that Act. This rate was generally described as the lower of 5 percent and the rate of earnings growth – although it was the Secretary of State who maintained the calculations tightly under his own control. We all now know that that escalation rate has been changed so that it now coincides with the limited price inflation rate originally written into section 52A of SSPA 1975 – the lower of 5 percent and the increase in the retail price index. When both inflation and earnings growth were running consistently above 5 percent, this severing of escalation's link to earnings meant nothing. But if earnings growth is now at or about 5 percent, and inflation only half that figure, the severing of that link has acquired a real significance.

Besides lower inflation-expectations, the second economic change our forward looking employer sees is European monetary union. We can be sure that it is going to happen, and that despite the pessimists it will have to be made to work (whatever the cost). The United Kingdom cannot remain unaffected, (we do not need for present purposes to define whether we will join, and if so when and on what terms). But in or out, our closeness to EMU countries, and the relationships we have with them, will make even more acute the problem still described only in the coded language that "our economic cycle is out of synch with that of the Continental economies". What that actually means is already visible in our gilt and bond markets, although these still have some way to move – that UK interest rates will need to fall to the levels of the Deutschmark bond markets.

So perhaps the actuarial assumptions we should be tending towards for the long term future would include:

6.5% valuation rate of interest

4.0% growth in the annuity fund – if annuity providers stubbornly insist on investing only in gilts

4.5% earnings growth

2.5% inflation.

If we recalculate the contributions that our employer would need to make, on the same funding assumptions, and to produce the same annuity as envisaged at the start of this article, the figures would be very different from what he had thought was adequate in the past:

7.00% for employees aged 25 to 34 (previously 3.75%)

12.00% for employees aged 35 to 44 (previously 7.50%)

20.25% for employees aged 45 to 54 (previously 14.25%)

33.75% for employees aged 55 to 64 (previously 26.25%).

The individual who leaves on his 35th birthday will have a fund by normal retirement age which will provide a 10/60ths pension based on a leaving salary escalated at 2.5 percent through the intervening 30 years – and the same will apply *mutatis mutandis* for an individual who leaves after 20, or 30 years.

The contributions are almost double the previous rates, because the rates of growth in fund (before as well as after retirement) are so much less. It is also worth noticing that if one fund is only to produce deferred pensions on a 2.5 percent escalation of leaving salary, the slope of the line becomes steeper – the cost of providing the final 10 years' pension for the man who remains in service becomes very high indeed.

But that is only a part of the story. We have, of course, not yet reached a conclusion that rates of return in the funds will fall as far, and as permanently, as we are envisaging; but let us continue with that assumption for the moment. The first individual whose contribution rates we considered at the beginning of this article would only be unaffected by changes in these rates of return if he and his widow are already dead. If he or his widow is still on pension, that will cost the employer's scheme more through the reduction in the annuity fund yield if the pension is self-provided, (or will hurt the insurance company if the pension has been purchased). And if the individual is still in service, his contributions to retirement will have to be substantially increased, whether his annuity is to be paid out of the scheme or purchased by it from an insurance company.

It is in the insurance companies' perspectives that some part of the problem can be seen to lie. It is not at all difficult to calculate that an annuity of the kind we have illustrated should be able to be purchased at an annuity rate of 6.7 percent (that is £100 of purchase price would provide £6.70 per annum pension for the individual) even if the yield in the fund is only 4 percent. If the fund can generate 5 percent yield, then the individual should have a pension of £7.20 per £100. But insurance companies are currently quoting annuity rates of around 6 percent, or less – hoping thus to recoup the losses they expect to incur on business already sold, yields having not only fallen, but being expected to fall further and then stay permanently low. So far as the occupational schemes are concerned, or for that matter the individuals providing pensions by money purchase, the insurance companies' prophecy is self fulfilling.

Changing, however an employer might do so, from final salary to money purchase could be no solution, unless the employer who made such a move was simply intending to give employees much smaller pensions in the future. One part of a solution might be a substantial reduction in the costs associated with pensions provision. This is self apparent in the personal pensions market, where the usual phraseology is that if pensions were bought rather than sold their costs could be dramatically reduced; but for both occupational and personal pension schemes, the costs of the degree of Inland Revenue and DSS regulation and control should not be underestimated – even if it is lost from view in the employer's own accounts. This is an area in which the NAPF's current moves to lighten the regulatory burden are most welcome.

In the medium term, one may also believe that many European states, including the United Kingdom, are going to have to improve their state pension provision. And that it will be acceptable in more instances than it has been to date for occupational schemes to cohabit, providing benefits designed to top up the state benefits to the aimed-at aggregate.

These are suggestions which may be of some small assistance at the margins; they cannot go very far towards meeting the significantly higher cost of pensions that the authors have come to believe will be the inevitable result of the economic changes we are living through, changes which as one thinks more about them look less and less likely to be reversible.

But all of the foregoing indicates an enormous opportunity available to be seized by any imaginative political leader. If compulsory saving is necessary, because universal, gratuitous state pension uplifts cannot be afforded; and if compulsory saving done through the institutions we have been discussing will give only the low benefit levels we have been discussing, why does government not undertake to boost the outcomes those savers could achieve? Then our occupational schemes could all cohabit entirely happily on top of the pensions that these compulsory state/private sector partnerships were able to produce.

David Wainman, *London*

Accounts, company

Companies need to account for the costs of pensions in their annual accounts. There have been two major changes in recent years. First, corporate governance has required the costs of pensions for directors to be specifically disclosed in the annual accounts. Secondly, the way in which overall costs are disclosed is now changing. Major changes in the guidelines are expected shortly, and they have been severely criticised especially by the actuarial profession which considers they will give a misleading impression in the accounts of the true position, and will be more volatile. The current guideline is SSAP 24, which allows flexible provisions and is actuary-friendly, allowing the use of long-term assumptions to smooth costs. The International Accounting Standards Committee issued in 1998 the new standard IAS 19 which employs the US standards set out in FAS 87. This uses market values, which are more volatile, and will lead to marked changes in the accounts from year to year. The point of the changes is to make it easier for shareholders to compare the performance of companies; the changes are understandable, and bring the United Kingdom into line with US practice, but are no more likely to make it easier to compare company with company, and could inflict unwelcome changes on investment policy, where long-term performance is sacrificed to the drive for lower volatility.

- Bacon & Woodrow, "Pension costs: the new accounting standards, a survey of FTSE 100 finance directors", 1998, 01372 733713.

Accounts, pension fund

Pension fund accounts are governed by the requirements of the Pensions Act 1995 and the SORP, statement of recommended practice, published by the Pensions Research Accountants Group. The continued relevance of the SORP is now under review by PRAG, especially in relation to the incorporation of AVC information, the loss of tax relief on UK equities, the valuation of securities, for which 'mid-market values' are no longer available (it is suggested that official closing prices should be used instead) and UITF (Urgent Issues Task Force) 20 abstract in relation to millenium issues. Dr Paul Klumpes of Lancaster University and Dr Stuart Manson of Essex University should report by mid-1999.

Actuarial valuations

Because of changes in ACT (advance corporation tax) many companies in which pension schemes are invested now return funds to investors not only by way of dividends but also through share buy-backs and other methods. The conventional method of valuing pension fund assets using dividend yields is therefore under pressure, and is expected to change fundamentally in the next few years, moving towards a market value basis, which may result however in more volatile valuations.

Additional voluntary contributions

See AVCs and FSAVCs.

Administration

Administration has become higher profile since the introduction of the compliance requirements of the Pensions Act 1995. There are now several books dedicated to the subject, the PMI organises a qualification in pensions administration, and the PRAG has a pensions audit discussion group which has issued a checklist.

- PRAG, *Pension Fund Administrators Control Environment, a Checklist for Trustees*, 15 October 1997
- PRAG, *Smaller Pension Schemes, Internal Controls: Fundamental Issues*, 28 November 1997
- Costs of administration are examined in the *Fifth Annual Pension Scheme Administration Survey*, Capita Hartshead, 01252 519255 (Alison Whitehead), £45
- A looseleaf manual is Tolley's *Pensions Administration*, 0181-686 9141, £125.

Appointment letters

The Pensions Act 1995 insists that certain advisers are formally appointed by the trustees of pension funds. There are problems beginning to emerge on such appointments. In particular, appointment of accountants and actuaries seems to involve trustees being required to give undertakings to their advisers, which was not the purpose of the legislation. The draft letters supplied by actuaries and accountants are usually unsatisfactory for trustees' purposes.

More recently it has been suggested that barristers acting for a pension fund must have a letter of appointment, which has struck some of them with horror; barristers would not know what a letter of engagement is. In practice unless a barrister is being used for day-to-day advice, it is improbable that such a letter is necessary.

Customer agreements or investment management agreements with asset managers cause considerable friction; best policy is to insist if possible on the standard agreement issued by the Institutional Fund Managers Association (IFMA) which is a fair and reasonable agreement and much shorter than most of the custom-made ones issued by the asset managers.

Arbitrage, fiscal and regulatory

The growing practice of selecting jurisdictions for their sympathetic fiscal or regulatory regimes. This is increasingly possible following the development of opportunities in the European Union. See also pan-European Pensions and Simplification

- Anthony Browne, "You can run but you can't hide, the OECD message for cut-price nations", *Observer*, 17 May 1998.

AVCs

See also FSAVCs.

Scheme members have the right to make additional voluntary contributions to their occupational scheme (Pension Schemes Act 1993 section 111). This enables them to buy additional or top-up benefits. Members cannot pay more than 15 percent of their earnings by way of AVCs, and in addition the usual Revenue limits apply.

- Pension Schemes (Voluntary Contributions Requirements and Voluntary and Compulsory Membership) Regulations 1987, SI 1987 No 1108.

Awards

We should all have prizes; current awards available, apart from special prizes granted by the Pensions Management Institute and Chartered Insurance Institute, include:

- *Pensions Management* awards (entries by July, lunch (lounge suit) in October) in association with the PMI; includes scheme of the year, pensions manager of the year, pensions personality of the year, trustee excellence and awards for schemes in different categories.
- *Professional Pensions* awards, April time, concentrate on pensions accountants, pensions personality and individual investments
- *Pensions Week* awards, also in the late Spring, devote themselves to communications, pensions managers and scheme of the year.

Cases

Introduction

Until relatively recently pension cases were pretty rare. This situation has changed dramatically, particularly in the last two years, a fact mainly attributable to Dr Farrand, the Pensions Ombudsman (*qv*). Aside from the cases heard in the European Court, Dr Farrand has played some part in the majority of pension cases heard in the last 12 months. With his robust approach to dispensing "cheap and cheerful" justice this is unlikely to change unless he finds that his wings were indeed judicially clipped in the case of *Edge* v *Pensions Ombudsman* which he is appealing as he fears the decision severely limits his jurisdiction. What follows is a brief selection of those cases which are thought likely to have a major impact on pension schemes.

TUPE/transfers

Although pension rights have always been expressly excluded from the protection afforded to employees transferred to a new employer under the Transfer of Undertakings (Protection of Employment) Regulations this has not prevented several attempts to persuade the courts otherwise. The decision in *Adams* v *Lancashire County Council* is the latest of these cases. The Council put its catering services out to tender and transferred its catering staff to the successful bidder, BET Catering Services Limited. The transferred employees who were no longer able to participate in the local government pension scheme found they were also ineligible to join BET's scheme. Their union, Unison, backed their claim that the EC Acquired Rights Directive required their pension entitlement to be protected in the same way as their general terms and conditions of employment. Both the High Court and Court of Appeal confirmed that the TUPE Regulations properly reflect the requirements of the Directive and there is no obligation on a new employer either to replicate or even offer pension provision to transferring employees. The only requirement is to ensure that accrued entitlement to the date of transfer is protected. This should for the time being lay this particular issue to rest, even though its effect is pretty harsh on employees who are transferred to new employers who decline to offer any pension provision at all.

Transfer payments

There have been several cases relating to members' requests for transfer payments. *Law Debenture* v *Pensions Ombudsman* turned on whether a member who requests a transfer payment before a scheme goes into wind-up can insist on it being paid in full after the wind-up procedures have commenced, even though it has become clear that there are insufficient funds available to pay transfer values in full for all deferred members. The Ombudsman thought that transfer payments should be paid in full in these circumstances – even though this would have entailed the remaining deferred members' benefits being scaled down even further. The High Court decided that the right to a transfer value could not take precedence over the winding-up priorities. Although some sympathy must be felt for those who requested transfer values before wind-up commenced it is unfair for those left behind to have to subsidise the few who had the foresight to jump ship before it began to sink.

Part-timers

From an employer's perspective, having won most of the battles it now looks as if the war over the inclusion of part-timers could well be lost. In *Magorrian* v *Eastern Health & Social Services* two mental health officers who had once worked full-time, claimed entitlement to a higher level of benefits payable to full-time mental health officers – which were denied to them as part-timers. Neatly getting round the Barber limitation on claims for retrospective entitlement the European Court decided that this was not a case about the level of benefits payable, but rather about access to benefits -which under the case of *Bilka Kaufhus* permitted backdating to 8 April 1976. It went on to find that the claim could not be limited to two years under UK legislation as this would render it impossible in practice for the individuals to enforce their rights under Community law. It is just possible that this case could be a one-off in that the circumstances were unique and the claims were submitted by the applicants while still in service with their employer. This meant that the issue of the UK time limit which requires claims to be brought within six months of leaving employment did not arise.

The House of Lords in *Preston* v *Wolverhampton Health Care Trust* – the lead part-timer case –

decided to refer the question of time limits to the European Court. It has requested guidance on whether the requirement to bring a claim under the Equal Pay Act 1970 within six months of leaving employment, and the restriction on backdating membership to two years, renders the exercise of rights conferred by Community law impossible in practice. Previously an Industrial Tribunal, the Employment Appeal Tribunal and the Court of Appeal had each ruled that UK limits are not incompatible with Community law so that there was no need to refer the question to the European Court. Following *Magorrian* the law lords concluded these questions should be referred to the European Court after all, although whether the issue will in fact be heard by the European Court is now open to question following the Advocate General's June 1998 opinion in *Levez*, indicating that a six-year limit would be more appropriate.

By chance, the Pensions Ombudsman has also grappled with the thorny issue of part-timers, deciding in *Shillcock* that barring entry to part-timers on the ground that their salary did not exceed the lower earnings limit (LEL) was indirectly discriminatory. Mrs Shillcock's salary rarely exceeded the LEL so she was denied access because the scheme operated an LEL deduction. Dr Farrand ordered three years backdated full membership subject to Mrs Shillcock paying the appropriate contributions: not a particularly helpful case for employers, which is likely to go to appeal. If a scheme operates an LEL deduction it may be prudent to offer part-timers a feeder scheme, such as a personal pension, or alternatively attempt to accommodate part-timers through a pro-rating arrangement.

Equality

The provision of benefits to same sex partners has received a judicial airing in the form of *Grant* v *South West Trains*. Whilst not a pension case it looked as if it might have implications for UK pension schemes after the Attorney General gave an opinion to the effect that it was unlawful to deny Miss Grant same sex partner travel concessions. The European Court declined to follow the Attorney General's opinion declaring instead that as comparable male employees were also denied the travel concessions for their same sex partners there was no discrimination based on sex. For the moment, at least, it looks as if the law on the provision of same sex partner benefits is settled but the position could change if the European Commission decide to issue a Directive on discrimination based on sexual orientation, which it is empowered to do under the Amsterdam Treaty.

The importance of the Booklet

The High Court in *Ward* v *ITN* in overturning a decision of the Ombudsman declared the scheme booklet a "highly abbreviated and generalised precis of the rules". ITN's booklet stated pension increases would be awarded at the rate of 4 percent per annum, but the rules permitted the trustees to pay lower increases. Dr Farrand had determined that the members were entitled to the increases stated in the booklet even though it said that the Scheme rules would prevail in cases of conflict between the two. The Court did, however, uphold the Ombudsman's award of compensation as the members had been misled. This decision is probably correct but don't expect the same result if the Rules have been incorrectly drafted and the booklet states the position correctly.

Surplus

Last but not least, there has been the usual crop of surplus cases, in which the ever present Ombudsman has played a leading role. Two of these cases are discussed briefly below. In *National Grid* two pensioners complained against the use of pension fund surplus to offset the pension cost of a redundancy programme. The Ombudsman sided with the pensioners but his decision was overturned in the High Court. There is little to be learned from the decision in terms of precedent value as the case was decided on a highly specific set of scheme rules. However, Mr Justice Robert Walker stated that it was a matter of "real public concern" that so much could turn on difficult and complex arguments relating to the correct interpretation of scheme rules and thought legislation might be needed. He added that a general exclusion of employers from surplus would lead to them paying the bare minimum to their pension schemes.

In *Edge* v *Pensions Ombudsman* the trustees agreed to reduce both employer and member contributions to reduce surplus. Pensioners complained that this was unjust as they received no benefit. The Ombudsman agreed and ordered the trustees to administer the scheme as if the reductions had not been introduced and to collect the back contributions from the employer and members – who were not represented. Not surprisingly, the decision was overturned on appeal. It was confirmed that the trustees can be partial provided they do not take account of irrelevant, irrational or improper factors. In an ongoing scheme it is not automatically improper for trustees to take into account the financial interest of the employer which may affect the future of the scheme. The case is most noteworthy for its relevance to the Ombudsman's jurisdiction. Employers should generally have a degree of control over the use of surplus. They have to dig deep if the scheme is in deficit and yet find themselves on the receiving end of an Ombudsman's complaint when they seek to benefit from surplus even though this goes hand in hand with benefit improvements. Perhaps the lesson is to ensure wherever possible that scheme documentation is clear on who has power to deal with surplus.

Conclusion

It is difficult to see, with the increasing number of complaints being handled by the Ombudsman, how the trend to litigate will diminish in the next 12 months. We have clearly not heard the last on many of the issues reviewed in this section, and next year the task of choosing which cases to comment upon will be harder still.

Ian Davies, *Cardiff*

Contracting-out

Contracting-out is a way of providing the second state pension benefits (SERPS) through a private arrangement, in exchange for paying lower national insurance contributions. The future of contracting-out is now somewhat in doubt, depending on where stakeholder pensions go, and whether there will be compulsory contributions to stakeholder pensions. For 1999–2000 there is no change to the NI rebate for COSRs (contracted-out salary related schemes) despite the additional costs imposed by the loss of the ACT credit on share dividends. The rebate is reduced for contracted-out money-purchase schemes to 2.2 percent (previously 3.1 percent), split 1.6 percent for the employee and 0.6 percent for the employer; there are age-related contributions for some employees. And controversially the rebate is increased for appropriate personal pensions, the personal pension version of contracted-out, where it is 3.8 percent (up from 3.4 percent) at the youngest ages, reducing for older ages.

The employer contracting-out rebate starts at £64 (1998) even though NI contributions start at £81 per week (1998).

It is clear therefore that the odds are stacked in favour of personal pensions, where the costs of appropriate group personal pensions are now attractive option for many employers.

There are concerns at present since the national insurance computer's new software, NIRS2, is not operational, and the Contracted-out Employments Group of the Contributions Agency (being merged with the Inland Revenue in April 1999) cannot give proper information about guaranteed minimum pension (GMP) liabilities to pension schemes. As a consequence, schemes are unable to comply with transfer requests within statutory time limits, or complete scheme wind-ups. At the same time, schemes are obliged to comply with the transfer request time limits under threat of OPRA penalties. Schemes and their advisers need to whistle-blow to OPRA if they cannot comply with transfer requests, but should explain the reason.

Corporate governance

Corporate governance is the increasingly important principle that shareholders should take more than just a simple financial interest in their shareholdings. The rise of the institutional shareholder, especially the pension fund shareholder, has meant that the balance of power between shareholder and management has swung in favour of management. An out-of-control management could pay itself well, use aeroplanes with abandon and lose sight of the fact that its job was to manage the company for the shareholders as well itself and others.

Corporate governance principles are now often expressed in customer agreements, so that investment managers are required to consider their votes (called "proxy votes") when they can. They often use services such as those provided by the NAPF Voting Issues Service (now linked with a US service ISS), or PIRC. Guidelines, now expressed in the Cadbury, Greenbury and Hampel codes, as well as in the Stock Exchange rules, have been consolidated (June 1998) in a Corporate Governance Supercode. Corporate governance should not be confused with ethical and social investments issues.

It is understood that only one UK fund manager has a full-time corporate governance office, namely Hermes.

- **www.calpers.ca.gov**
- **www.corpgov.net**
- Dr Matthew Gaved, "Institutional investors and corporate governance: proposals for a code of disclosure", Foundation for Business Responsibilities, 01753 537171, March 1998, £5
- Voting services: NAPF Voting Issues Service; PIRC Ltd; Manifest Voting Agency; Date Source Ltd; Association of British Insurers
- Matthew Craig, "Casting a vote for UK PLC", *Pensions Management*, May 1998, p39.

Data protection

At one time it was thought that trustees of a pension fund could avoid registration under the Data Protection Act 1984; section 32 exempted pensions data. Following the Pensions Act 1995, the Data Protection Registry considers that trustees are a separate legal entity and should now register. The Data Protection Act 1998 which reflects the EU Data Protection Directive (95/46/EC) also seems to cover waiting period members or those covered only for life cover. It also covers non-computer records. Trustees should register as an unincorporated body or, if corporate, separately from the employer. If there are several schemes, it is the trustees not the schemes which register.

- Karen Aveyard, "The protection racket" [1998] *Pensions World* 29.

Disclosure

Disclosure is the right of members to certain information about their scheme. Certain schemes are exempt (one man schemes, death-benefit only schemes), and active members, deferred pensioners and pensioners are covered; there is some doubt about divorcing spouses. Schemes can charge reasonable copying and postage costs to members for some of the bulkier information. The rules on disclosure are now complex.

- Disclosure regulations can be tracked on **www.watsonwyatt.com/uk/uk** as well as on *Perspective.*

Dispute resolution

Recent years have seen increased difficulties for employers and pension fund trustees raised by:

- the increase in the number of dispute resolution options over the last few years;
- the changes in approach to pensions law and practice (often retrospective) by judicial and quasi-judicial authorities which have involved

a growing number of employers in expensive legal disputes, with an increasing need to become involved in appeals;

- the growing number of "palm-tree test cases" , the decisions which are often made in a manner which, while acceptable when resolving an individual matter, may be inappropriate where it has significant implications when applied across a wider membership;
- the growing number of decisions which while apparently in favour of an individual, may paradoxically adversely affect the membership as a whole in the longer run (for example, cases involving allocation of surplus);
- the imbalance of risk between fund member and employer/trustee, since complaints can now be made without risk to the complainant while involving the defendant in substantial costs.

Dispute resolution system in the pensions area

It is normally recognised that pension disputes can be expensive and protracted. This was the thinking behind the suggestion of the Occupational Pensions Board some years ago that a dispute resolution system specifically designed for pension funds and pension scheme members be introduced. The recommendation of the OPB was for a pensions tribunal, along the lines of an industrial tribunal, with a lawyer as chairman, and two technical assessors, for the resolution of disputes in which individual members of schemes would be unable to pursue because of the risk as to costs.

In the event, for a number of political reasons, the Department of Social Security recommended the introduction of a Pensions Ombudsman. For a number of years this worked reasonably satisfactorily, in association with OPAS, on a low key basis, although the Pensions Ombudsman was criticised in the past for too low a profile.

Changes to the system

There have been, however, some changes to the system in recent years, which may indicate the need for a review of the current dispute resolution arrangements.

First, some years ago the Ombudsman's office became more interventionist, and as a consequence there have been substantial numbers of appeals from his determinations in recent years, many of which have been successful.

Secondly, in the meantime an additional dispute resolution system has been introduced through the operation of the Pensions Act 1995, namely an internal dispute resolution system, so that private complainants now have what could be perceived to be an excess of remedy:

- an internal complaint;
- an appeal on an internal complaint;
- a reference to OPAS;
- a reference to the Pensions Ombudsman;
- an application through the normal judicial system.

Problems of current arrangements

There are a number of issues which now arise in relation to the present system:

- whether the balance between the protection of the individual and the liability of the trustees/employers is correct;
- whether the principles underlying the establishment of pension schemes, in relation for example to employers' duties, ownership of surplus and trustee liabilities is being enforced in the way anticipated, or current systems attempt to create new law rather than interpret it;

- whether it is possible to devise a simpler, more cost-effective system, reflecting both the needs of the industry and protection of the individual in a better form.

A question of balance

The question now arises whether the dispute resolution system that is in place for pensions contains the correct balance between giving the consumer an adequate remedy to pursue an injustice, and the ability of an individual consumer to "blackmail" an employer so that it is cheaper to settle than to fight.

Complaints can be made by an individual without risk as to costs or liability which can involve employers and trustees in very substantial defence costs; the possibility of nuisance claims is therefore very much enhanced.

New law: test cases

It is clear that decisions emerging from the Pensions Ombudsman's Office may be developing new principles of law, or perhaps reverting to older principles of trust law which do not apply to pensions trusts.

Resolving these general principles is now involving UK employers in significant costs which were not anticipated when the Ombudsman's Office was established. The problem is that single cases, in pensions terms, are usually not ring-fenced and can often have significant implications for many other members, sometimes many thousands of other members.

The Pensions Ombudsman himself is concerned about the costs and delays in appeals and has called for such appeals to be constrained by law. The question arises whether a Pensions Ombudsman system is appropriate for developing these general principles when it was designed for assisting in the resolution of simple disputes.

The knock-on effect

The original dispute resolution system was intended to resolve individual disputes involving what are relatively small amounts (ie important to the consumer individually, but not significant to the pension schemes). The particular difficulty in pension schemes is the disproportionately large knock-on effect that small individual disputes can now have on the employer/pension scheme since they affect so many individuals and are multiplied therefore many times over. A particular example, not in the pensions sphere, is the case of *Wolfe* v *Department of National Savings*, in which an individual, who had invested £20,000 in National Savings certificates, complained that in a leap year she was entitled to an additional one day's interest worth £2.73. Although the case individually was hardly worth fighting, the actual decision would have involved many tens of millions of £.

Existing research

There is a limited amount of research available on pensions disputes; the DSS has already (1997) issued a research document on pensions disputes which does not, however, cover the issues raised here and the Pensions Ombudsman has conducted a great deal of private research on the pros and cons of ombudsman procedures as opposed to tribunal procedures.

Possible reforms

Reforms (all of which may have their own drawbacks) could include:

- establishing an alternative dispute resolution system (mediation);
- reducing the number of available procedures;
- establishing a pensions tribunal as an alternative to the Ombudsman;
- introducing a more limited right of appeal by either parties or the Pensions Ombudsman or both;

- introducing a risk element, so that complainants might have to put up a modest security for costs (perhaps £100 or £250) unless it was certified fit for complaint by, say, OPAS;
- restricting the role of the Pensions Ombudsman by in particular prohibiting the support of test cases for developing the law;
- prohibiting the reporting of decisions, which would avoid Pensions Ombudsman's decisions being regarded as precedents and thus needing appeal.

Divorce

The "earmarking" orders which pension funds have been subject to since August 1996 have proved something of a damp squib; by August 1998 scarcely 300 orders had been made. So the impact on the administration and management of pension funds has, in that respect been modest. However, there are increasing requests for "cash-equivalent transfer values" (CETVs) which schemes are obliged to render, and by April 2000 schemes will have to comply with "sharing" (formerly "splitting") orders. Earmarking orders must be registered by the pension scheme and transferred with any transfers to other schemes. Schemes may object to orders which cannot be complied with and parties are being urged to clear the terms of their orders before having them sealed by the court.

Divorcing couples will eventually have three choices:

- *set-off*, (as before) under which there is a division of assets to take account of pension rights;
- *earmarking*, which has just come into force, which allows division of pension payments at retirement; and
- *sharing*, which may come into force over the next few years, which allows division of cash equivalents at divorce.

So far as pension funds are concerned, there are some oddities about the reforms. Divorce advisers are not so far reknowned for their pensions expertise, and so the reforms operate on the principle of simplicity. One of those simplifications is that of valuation of pension rights. In principle, there should be no need for complex and expensive valuations: it is not the capital value of the pension that is needed, since it cannot, (yet) be split. But the regulations require the affidavit of means to disclose the value of pension rights — and prescribe a method of valuation. That method is known as the cash equivalent transfer value. But that simple, free, valuation is only part of the story, and its disclosure does not enable the parties to have sufficient information to decide how they should deal with the pension rights.

Member's valuations The value of a member's or an employee's rights in a money-purchase pension system is (theoretically) relatively easy to identify; it is (except as below) the value of the assets standing to his credit. The value of an employee's interests in a final-salary is more difficult to define, since it involves the application of actuarial techniques, identifying the value of the underlying guarantee, and the impact of the imprecise value of discretionary benefits. There is, however, a standard valuation technique, called a "cash-equivalent", based on recommended actuarial guidance, which is used by the regulations. This is discussed below.

Spouse's valuations The value of a spouse's rights is a proportion of a member's rights. But a spouse's interest is in several parts, particularly in respect of salary-related schemes:

- the survivor's rights, which disappear by virtue of any divorce; and
- the interest in the member's rights which he enjoys once the benefit is in payment.

There is some actuarial interest in discretionary or contingent benefits; but lump sums (except as a means of future payment) are only a different way of expressing a pension benefit (this is slightly different in the case of some public sector schemes). The interest will be affected or can be affected by a number of elements including:

- the life expectancy of the member; if that is impaired, the spouse's interest will be greater;
- the difference in ages of the spouses; if the spouse is much younger, her interest could be greater.

It is often convenient to express a spouse's rights as a percentage of a member's rights.

Methods available

Pension fund managers (though not all divorce lawyers) know that there are many ways of valuing a member's interests. In money-purchase cases the value of the account is often easy to determine. But even here, there may be a different value depending on whether the funds are left with the investment manager or insurer (the "fund value") or whether the policy is to be paid up or surrendered (the "surrender value"), which could be very substantially less. The rules require the surrender value to be used as the default value, which clearly is often to the disadvantage of the spouse.

In defined-benefit cases, as well as the problems of what benefits to take into account, and the variability of the personal factors, there are problems of assumptions. There are two main assumption problems:

First, the fact that assumptions as to future interest rates, income rates and annuity rates can be difficult to agree. Few can guess as to future inflation rates for example; and low future inflation could double the value of a benefit compared with high future inflation. Different actuaries will have different expectations about these future rates, and small differences in assumptions can have major differences in valuations. It is sensible to use mid-range assumptions, regardless of whether the valuation is prepared for the petitioner or the respondent, but in particular cases these may not be appropriate.

Secondly, the fact that defined-benefit schemes often contain reserves designed to cope with the fact that a member may continue in employment with the company and that he may enjoy salary increases and career progression increases. If the member leaves before they come into play, those reserves are no longer required.

It is therefore possible to value the same pension rights in many different ways; the three most commonly referred to include:

- past service reserves, which include the reserves mentioned above;
- transfer values (or sometimes cash equivalents) a statutory minimum valuation, which does not take into account these reserves; or
- share of fund, which if there is a significant surplus in the fund, may be higher than the first two (or lower, if there is a deficit in the fund).

Cash equivalent transfer value

The regulations (the Divorce etc (Pensions) Regulations 1996) require that the valuation method used in the proceedings is the cash equivalent transfer value (CETV). It was the method recommended by the Pensions Management Institute/Law Society Working Party Report of 1993. Its advantage is that it is cheap (free) to the parties and readily calculable (in principle) by pension schemes. Its drawback is that it is sometimes much lower than the "fund value" or "past service reserve", sometimes only a fifth of the full value. Another way of looking at it is to distinguish between what the transfer value is and what the cost of buying equivalent benefits is.

Where the parties have been married for some time, or the earnings are higher, such a valuation can be misleading, sometimes by a factor of four or five. In such cases it is crucial and prudent to use a different system, perhaps the past service reserve approach, which may be more appropriate. It certainly enables the solicitor to give proper advice on which method of settlement should be employed. In many cases the simple CETV does not provide sufficient information to the client to decide whether to try to achieve either set-off or earmarking — and whichever method, what the amounts should be.

Powers of the court

From 1 July 1996 the court has had power to make an order in respect of pensions. In relation to petitions issued before July, although it was settled law that the court could take pensions into account when considering financial arrangements on divorce (and in Scotland had to consider pensions) in practice the law throughout the United Kingdom was constrained by the fact that the courts had no authority to direct pension scheme managers and trustees to allocate one spouse's interests or part of them to another. In practice, there were two main problems:

- that the court had no power to make an order in relation to a member's pension rights; and
- that it was difficult in some cases for a spouse's adviser to obtain the information.

But sharing has its problems too (as the Green Paper on splitting mentioned some years ago). First, it would often be more tax efficient for couples who are living amicably with each other to divorce, split the pension and pay a lower tax rate on each part of the pension. Married couples would argue, with some justification, that this amounts to a tax on marriage. Second, contracted-out rights would be subject to sharing whereas contracted-in would not. Splitting, now known as sharing, will allow the division of SERPs benefits as well as private pension arrangements; it is expected to be in force by April 2000, so that schemes will have to make arrangements permitting either transfers out of part of a member's rights or permitting a former spouse to be admitted a member of the scheme.

Trustees are now entitled to receive, once an earmarking order has been made, a copy of the court application, details of the address to which they may be required to send information about the scheme and sufficient details of a bank account or an address to which payments should be sent if an earmarking order is made.

Meanwhile matrimonial and family lawyers are faced with the new problem of explaining the pros and cons of the new options to their clients — and making sure there is a letter on file to ensure that when their clients make the wrong choice, as with hindsight they will, their files are claim proof. Pension funds will be faced with the prospect that not only will they have to amend their administration and computer systems to cope with the existing reforms (so that they do not inadvertently pay benefits to a member instead of to a former spouse), but also amend them yet again to cope with the prospect of sharing, so as to be able to make spouses and former spouses members of schemes. The cost of these changes will not be insignificant; the irony is that in practice so far very few earmarking orders against schemes have been made in the two years they have been available — and the prospect is that very few sharing orders either will be sought. Choice is proving a mixed blessing, but at least it will keep the software guys busy.

Ingrid Everson, *Birmingham*

- Julia Field & Gillian Prior, Women and Pensions, Department of Social Security Research Report No 49, HMSO, July 1996,ISBN 0-11-762422-5, £35
- Gillian Prior & Julia Field, Pensions and Divorce, Department of Social Security Research Report No 50, HMSO, July 1996, ISBN 0-11-762423-3, £25
- Matrimonial Causes Act 1973 sections 25, 25A, 25B, 25C, 25D and 31
- Pensions Act 1995 sections166 and 167
- Lord Chancellor's Department, Summary Paper: The Provisions of the Regulations under

section 166 of the Pensions Act 1995, June 1996

- The Divorce etc (Pensions) Regulations 1996, SI 1996 No 1676
- The Family Proceedings (Amendment) (No 2) Rules 1996, SI 1996 No 1674 (L3)
- The Family Proceedings (Amendment) (No 3) Rules 1996, SI 1996 No 1778 (L4)
- The Pensions Act (Commencement) (No 5) Order 1996, SI 1996 No 1675 (C36)
- Department of Social Security, No quick fix legislation for pensions splitting on divorce vows Lord MacKay (sic), Press Release, 29 July 1996
- Department of Social Security, The Treatment of Pension Rights on Divorce, Command Paper 3345, HMSO, July 1966, £14.80
- Robin Ellison & Keith Popplewell, “Pensions and divorce”, a video, Eagle Star, July 1996
- A copy of the consolidated regulations and guidance for matrimonial lawyers is available free on request from The Divorce Corporation, 0114-262 0616
- Robin Ellison & Maggie Rae, Family Breakdown and Pensions, Butterworths, 1997
- DSS, Pension Sharing on Divorce, 2 vols, June 1998.

Early retirement

The PSO impose strict rules on early retirement; normally retirement before age 50 is not permitted except in the case of certain high risk jobs. The Revenue is also much exercised about retirement and subsequent employment while drawing a pension. After considerable complaints in 1998 about strict rules on not retiring and then resuming work, it is understood the rules are under reconsideration.

In practice early retirement poses a risk for employees since not only could inflation still affect pension values if it exceeds 5 percent per annum, especially since many schemes only protect accruals after 1996; and few match increases in living standards.

Only 42 percent of men aged between 55 and 64 are in work, compared with 75 percent 20 years ago. More than 75 percent of all local authority employees retire early at an average age of 54, 40 percent because of ill-health, costing £35,000 per employee, a total of £5.7 billion over the six years to 1996. As a consequence local authority contributions rose from 4 percent of payroll in 1992 to 9 percent in 1998, rising to 12 percent by 2000. Police and firemen's schemes reduced early retirement rights in 1998.

- Incomes Data Services, May 1998; Institute for Fiscal Studies; Audit Commission, Retiring Nature, November 1997.

Equal treatment

Most of the concern in recent years has been not on the broad outline of equal treatment in pension schemes, mostly settled in the *Barber & Coloroll* cases, but on some of the detail, especially in relation to the extent of claims that part-timers might make. Two cases *(Preston* v *Wolverhampton Healthcare and Levez*) before the European Court of Justice explore whether part-timers who have been discriminated against can claim back for more than the two years that the Pensions Act 1995 provides; an Advocate General's opinion in Levez suggests that six years might be the appropriate period.

Shillcock is a case on appeal from the Pensions Ombudsman, whose determination held that excluding employees below the lower earnings limit from scheme membership was discrimination, because it was mostly women who were on this low income Although it was unlikely that they would have enjoyed improved pension benefits they were excluded from death cover.

- *Levez* v *T H Jennings (Harlow Pools) Ltd* (ECJ, Advocate General's opinion, June 1998)

- *Preston* v *Wolverhampton Healthcare Trust* [1998] PLR 39 (HL)
- *Maggorian* v *Eastern Health* [1998] PLR 1
- *Shillcock* v *Uppingham School* [1997] PLR 204.

Euro

By the year 2002 only the Euro will be legal tender in 11 out of the 15 EU Member states: Austria, Belgium, Finland, France, Germany, Ireland, Italy, Luxembourg, Netherlands, Portugal, and Spain. But some transitional changes have already taken place from 1 January 1999. The NAPF suggested that schemes will need to review their administrative procedures, especially if they have multi-national subsidiaries in the Euro zone, if they have pensioners in the Euro zone or if they have members seconded to work in a Euro zone country with a Euro denominated salary.

No-one is exactly sure what the impact of the Euro within Europe will have on pension funds. There is a PRAG working party examining the issue and the NAPF has issued a very useful guide. The main concern, apart from the obvious though minor ones of enforcement of contracts, is what RPI rate should be applied to benefit increases, since internal inflation in individual Member States will differ widely.

- *Euro: Implications for Pension Schemes*, NAPF, 0171-730 0585, May 1998, ISBN 0-905796 69 1, £10
- *Euro Audit for Scheme Administrators*, NAPF, 0171-730 0585, 1998, £6
- *The Euro: a Short Checklist for Trustees*, PRAG
- *The Euro and Pensions: a Guide to EMU for Irish Pension Scheme Trustees,* Irish Association of Pension Funds, 00353 1661 2427
- *Euro Scenario – Manual for the Implementation of the Euro by Pension Funds*,

Foundation for Company Pension Funds (Netherlands), [in English], 0031 703 490190.

European Union

Mobility Directive

A draft Directive on mobility of scheme members has been agreed by the EU. This will enable employees to protect their pension rights when moved between Member States as part of their employment. Workers will be able to stay in their home state scheme if they are posted to another Member State for a short period and there will be facilities for cross-border payment of pensions.

Green Paper

A Green Paper proposed by Commissioner Mario Monti in July 1997 proposed a directive controlling pension funds throughout the EU. The Directive will not cover taxation issues.

- DSS Press Release, 4 June 1998
- Proposal for a Council Directive on safeguarding the supplementary pension rights of employed and self-employed persons moving within the Community, 11325/97 SOC 302 COM 97(486) final.

FSAVCs

See also AVCs.

FSAVCs or free standing additional voluntary contributions rely on the fact that scheme members are required by law to have access to the right to pay AVCs (additional voluntary contributions). “Free-standing” means that they can be paid to someone other than the scheme. They are tricky to administer, and in 1998 it was suggested that anyone who sold an FSAVC had to be mis-selling because the charges are much higher. The PIA is conducting an investigation into the alleged mis-selling, although independent financial advisers still consider that FSAVCs are attractive.

- Free Standing Additional Contributions Supplement, Inland Revenue, IR12(1979) Supp 8/89 3rd ed
- Darren McLauchlan, "Unloved but not unnecessary", *Financial Adviser*, 4 June 1998.

FURBs

Funded Unapproved Retirement Benefit Schemes (FURBs) were effectively created by the introduction of an "earnings cap" in 1989, which set a limit on the amount of earnings in respect of which contributions may be paid into a tax-approved pension scheme. FURBs are designed to enable an employer (less commonly) to secure future benefit rights through an insurance policy, such as in death-benefit schemes, or to set up a separate trust fund specifically for participating members,

The Contributions Agency believes that some FURBs are established not bona fide to provide retirement benefits but as a national insurance contributions avoidance measure; they have alleged that some "alleged schemes" are set up with the sole purpose of deferring a payment of earnings to a future date in a disguised format in the belief that it escapes NI contribution liability. It gives the example of a scheme where the employer sets up a trust for an individual employee (perhaps the company director) into which a lump sum is paid, equivalent to the annual bonus. Rather than using the money paid in to provide a pension, the trustees pay the money out to the employee a few days or weeks later. The CA say that they have always reserved the right to charge NI contributions where a FURB is used not to provide pensions but to pay bonuses. In November 1997 a CA Press Release was issued to clarify the CA's approach.

The NAPF believe that the imposition of such NICs is a breach of the equal treatment provisions of the Treaty of Rome, since more women than men have a break in their private pensions record, and can only catch up by means of a FURB.

It is also not yet certain whether capital gains tax provisions introduced by the Finance Act 1998 apply to capital gains made by a FURB, since a FURB does not seem to be treated as a "settlement". The Act was intended to increase the CGT rate from 23 percent to 34 percent as from 6 April 1998.

It may be therefore that FURBs still maintain an attractive role; while the individual bears tax on the contributions made into a FURB, the FURB pays income tax only at the basic rate on its earnings, may not pay capital gains tax, the employer receives tax relief on the contributions in, and the benefits (to maintain fiscal equality) are paid tax free as a lump sum at retirement. It is usually inadvisable to pay the benefits as a pension, since such pension is taxed again.

- Contributions Agency, Press Release,17 November 1997
- *National Insurance News*, Issue 10, Spring 1998 Funded Unapproved Retirement Benefit Schemes
- Social Security Act 1998 section 48, together with regulations published and effective by 6 April 1999 which apportion payments into FURBs made for the benefit of two or more employed earners
- Finance Act 1998.

Group personal pension plans

GPPPs are enjoying a growing popularity as an alternative to occupational money-purchase schemes. The main advantage is the lower compliance costs, since GPPPs are not governed by the Pensions Act 1995; the disadvantage is that they are subject to the Financial Services Act 1986, so that they must be administered by an authorised person, such as a pensions consultant, and the employer cannot become as involved. There is now quite an expertise, however, in branding GPPPs as a form of company sponsored plan. More modern arrangements separate the administration from the investment much as self-administered company schemes, and allow a full selection of investment choice to the member; they are growing almost indistinguishable from the SIPP (*qv*). If a non-commission system can be devised, GPPPs can be attractive to employers; there are no member-trustee requirements and disclosure is covered by the Personal Pension Schemes (Disclosure) Regulations 1987, SI 1987 No 1110. There is debate about whether for TUPE (*qv*) purposes a GPPP "sponsored" by an employer is an "occupational scheme" as defined in the Pension Schemes Act 1993 (and therefore exempt from the TUPE rules) or not. If it is, it may be subject to the Pensions Act requirements, which was not what was intended.

- Chris Bellers, (London & Manchester) "Working out the IFAs commission", *Investment Week*, 11 May 1998.

Industry-wide schemes

Industry-wide schemes seem to be falling in popularity, despite their apparent advantages: pooling of costs and risks and an ability for people working within the same industry to move jobs without suffering losses on transfers. There are now about 1.6 million members of such schemes in the United Kingdom (they are much more popular in other countries, especially France, for example). In recent years administration has caused problems and OPRA is particularly exercised about late payment of contributions from such schemes, which is inevitable where many smaller employers are having to send in individual payments. It may be that industry-wide schemes will have a fresh burst of popularity once stakeholder is on its way, as trade unions and others may be prompted to establish them.

Investments

Ethical investments

There seems to be a trend towards ethical investment in pension funds, although few fund managers seem geared up to it, and many employers and trustees are somewhat suspicious of the costs involved. It is difficult to justify ethical investment at the expense of members, if there is an expense, and there are conflicts of just what is ethical. Legal constraints however seem to have loosened since the rather extreme decision in *Copwan* v *Scargill* in 1984.

- Ethical Investment Research Service, "73% want ethical pension funds", 7 June 1998.

Investment management

One of the great curses of investment management is the jargon the other being the often unacceptable investment management agreements. There are now standards, and scheme managers and others should insist on the use of the standards now agreed within the industry, rather than house-style drafts. Over time it should be possible both to persuade investment houses to use the standard largely unchanged, and save several thousand pounds on legal fees on checking them.

- Hymans Robertson, *Glossary of Investment Management Terms*, 64pp, free 0171-831 9561
- IFMA/LIBA, *Standard Investment Management Agreement Version 3b*, with explanatory notes.

Kitemarking

Because of the personal pension mis-selling episode, any introduction of stakeholder pensions would need an additional raft of consumer protection if the complexity of the existing system is to be avoided. It must be avoided if sales to lower earners are not to be disproportionately expensive.

Accordingly it has been suggested that certain pension products should be given a government kitemark, which would signal that they were good value for money, and safe. There are two main problems with the idea; first, they might give a spurious guarantee of value for money and competitive performance. Secondly, it may be illegal under EU law (3rd Life Directive). It would, however, offer an opportunity for the government to prefer those providers not involved in the previous mis-selling episode, which may not only be discriminatory in itself, but also outlaw some of the better providers.

- John Hughes, Head of Pensions Review Team of the DSS, "Benchmarking Stakeholder Pensions", paper to Westminster City Conference, 3 July 1998.

Liability

See OPDU.

Loans

Loans to members are controlled by the Inland Revenue (forbidden in the case of SSASs and SIPPs) and guidance is set out on what trustees and insurers are expected to do to manage permitted loans

- PSO Update 43.

Maternity

The Department of Trade and Industry confirms that employers must continue paying contributions to an employee's personal pension whilst she is on unpaid statutory maternity leave. Unless there is an express provision within the contract of employment, the Employment Rights Act does not appear to require the employer also to pay the employee's contribution.

Minimum funding requirement

Pension funds which promise salary-related benefits are required to have minimum funds to support the promise. The amount of those funds is derived from actuarial guidance set out in a Guidance Note issued by the Faculty and Institute of Actuaries, GN27. The original valuation assumptions had to be changed in June 1998 because of changes in (reductions in) gross dividend yield in recent years partly because of changes to ACT (advance corporation tax). The effect of these changes has been to reduce the normal transfer values as well as easing the sums required by schemes to be maintained as assets.

- GN 27
- Letter from Institute and Faculty of Actuaries, 15 June 1998.

Mobility Directive

See European Union.

OPAS

OPAS is the Occupational Pensions Advisory Service, a non-profit organisation funded by the DSS via OPRA, intended to offer a useful free advisory service to individuals complaining about their occupational pensions. Since the introduction of internal dispute resolution (IDR) its services have come under less pressure, but it is still a handy pressure valve.

There is even a history of OPAS launched in 1998. Lots of other free publications available: see addresses.

OPDU

See also Trustees.

With the increased exposure of trustees, employers and advisers to liability both for breach of trust and of statutory breaches under the Pensions Act 1995, steps have been taken by most pension funds and their sponsors to limit liability as much as possible. Initial steps include:

- exclusion of liability clauses in the deeds; these clauses have received judicial approval in recent cases, and best practice suggests that the simpler the clause the better;
- indemnity clauses in the deed so that trustees' and others' liabilities are picked up either by the trust itself or the employer;

- incorporation of the trustees into a limited liability company; again this practice has received judicial approval in recent years.

However, none of these is an absolute guarantee, and there are two main problems in practice. First, liability may occur some time after an individual has left the fund or the employer; secondly, there may be substantial legal fees incurred in defending claims which in the end are dismissed. The Occupational Pensions Defence Union (OPDU), managed by a supervisory body of its members, is designed to protect individuals for up to 10 years after they have left, regardless of whether there is a conflict of interest with other members, trustees or employers. OPDU offers insurance, like other insurance protection schemes, but also manages claims and protects so far as possible against fines and penalties.

OPRA

Occupational Pensions Regulatory Authority supervises compliance with the provisions of the Pensions Act 1995. It is clear that OPRA is concentrating on breaches involving late payment of contributions, in respect of which it is firmer than the government is in relation to recovery of PAYE and NI payments. Concerns are also growing in relation to appeal procedures, especially following the introduction of the provisions of the European Convention on Human Rights, which make it inappropriate for the same body to have both investigative, prosecutorial and judicial powers, and in relation to penalties imposed in SSASs and pensioneer trustees which some regard as disproportionate.

Annual reports and regular bulletins indicate progress and set out guidelines. Information is available direct and from the website.

- Interview with John Hayes, Chairman, by Joanne Gill, *Financial Adviser*, 21 May 1998
- OPRA, Invicta House, Trafalgar House, Brighton BN1 4DW 01273 627600, website **www.opra.gov.uk.**

Pan-European pension schemes

There has been pressure for several years, indeed ever since Sir Leon Brittan, a European Commissioner, delivered a speech in 1991 calling for such schemes, for a pan-European pension scheme to be available under EU rules. The tax authorities in most Member States objected, but the trend of decisions in the European Court of Justice, in particular the Bachmann case, the Wieloxck case and most recently the *Safir* case (in April 1998) seems to indicate that a pan-European pension scheme is now possible. Not only that, which would be attractive to employers with employees in several Member States, and moving between those states, but it would allow a company based solely in, say, the United Kingdom to set up a scheme in, say, Ireland, because for example the regulatory regime was less oppressive. It seems likely that following yet another series of decisions, *Schjindel* and *Fédération Française* in relation to whether a pension scheme is an enterprise or a social security system, and Clean Car Autoservice on whether a regulator can object on the ground of foreign residence, that it will be perhaps only a matters of a few years before pan-European pension schemes will be here. The implications are that many of the existing Revenue rules would not apply, especially in relation to retirement ages and accrual rates, and much of the OPRA regulation could be by-passed. It is expected that a test case will be filed shortly.

- *Bachmann* v *Belgium* [1995] PLR 219
- *Safir* [1998] PLR 181
- *Wielockx* v *Inspecteur der Directe Belastingen* [1995] PLR 203
- *Fédération Française des Sociétés d'Assurance* v *Ministère de l'Agriculture et de la Pêche* [1996] PLR 89
- *Clean Car Autoservice GsmbH* v *Landeshauptmann von Wien*, ECJ Case - 350/96 Times Law Report, 13 May 1998.

Pensions Ombudsman

The Pensions Ombudsman system is intended to allow individuals who otherwise would find it impossible to press complaints because the costs would be too high to make a claim. Discussion about the role of the Pensions Ombudsman's office continues because it is the only Ombudsman service which has the power of enforcement, and to award penalties for distress and inconvenience. It can also make decisions which, while limited to an individual's rights, might have major implications when spread over all the members of the scheme, so that millions could be involved. There is also discussion about whether the office has treated the nature of surpluses in accordance with industry practice. The Inland Revenue has objected to the office making awards for distress, saying that it is improper for funds to pay such sums, and in some cases awards against trustees are payable by the fund. In a closed fund, this can have an effect on the rights of the remaining members.

- Mark Grant, *The Pensions Ombudsman*, Sweet & Maxwell, July 1998, ISBN 075200 6037, £125.

Personal pensions

See also Group personal pensions.

Mis-selling

In 1986 many insurers and others (known as pension providers) and intermediaries sold personal pension arrangements to members and potential members of occupational schemes. After a review by the Securities and Investments Board in 1994 it was considered that many of these sales were improper, because they did not involve "best advice". Occupational schemes are under no obligation to receive back those employees who opted out, but the majority of the larger schemes do, provided they receive enough funds to ensure other members are not affected. Schemes may charge reasonable amounts to prepare the estimates for insurers.

PFPVs

Pension Fund Pooling Vehicles were designed by the Inland Revenue as a response to competition from European investment managers, and to ensure tax transparency for pension fund investors. Their use has been minimal to date, although this may increase as the impact of the removal of ACT increases. Managed funds, for example, are now being translated into PFPVs intended to avoid certain stamp duty and other fiscal costs.

Part-timers

See also Equal Treatment; Cases.

A separate Directive extends the part-time work Directive to the United Kingdom; it takes effect in the United Kingdom by 7 April 2000 so that part-timers must enjoy pro-rata benefits by then. So far as occupational pension rights are concerned, such rights already seem to be protected by decisions of the European Court in decisions such as *Bilka-Kaufhaus* and others, the only question being how far back such rights extend.

Policy

Pension policy has been subjected to a battery of studies, following the government's declared intention to introduce Stakeholder pensions (*qv*). Several studies indicate however that the much disliked SERPS scheme is still considered preferable, perhaps amended to be funded, and to simplify or abolish contracting-out.

- ABI, Issues Concerning UK Pension Policy, 51 Gresham Street London EC2V 7HQ 0171-600 3333, June 1998.

Proxy voting

See also Corporate governance.

Shares that pension schemes own carry not only a capital value and a dividend, but also a vote. US pension schemes are required under their legislation and US guidelines ("the Avon letter") to consider voting all their shares, although they may abstain. The US influence has percolated into the United Kingdom, where many schemes now mandate their asset managers to exercise the votes on their behalf. Further details are set out under the Corporate governance entry.

Retirement

The Inland Revenue for reasons which seem obscure insists that scheme members retire before they draw benefits; the need for this is under discussion. Meanwhile, the academics have been studying how and when individuals retire and have come to the astonishing conclusion that older pensioners are poorer than younger ones.

Oddly, the invention of retirement discourages people from staying in work, which the OECD considers is wrong, since it may condemn older people to unemployment.

- "The dynamics of incomes and occupational pensions after retirement"; "The dynamics of male retirement"; "Asset wealth and asset decumulation among households in the retirement survey" all in [1998] *Fiscal Studies*, 0171- 291 4800, £8.

- "Growing old extravagantly", *The Economist*, 20 June 1998; Social Security programs around the world, NBER Working Paper 6134; Maintaining prosperity in an aging society, OECD, April 1998; Sveinborn Blondal & Stefano Scarpetta, "Retire early, stay at work?", *OECD Observer*, June/July 1998.

Scotland

Scotland has a different law, although most of pensions law is the same as the rest of the United Kingdom. Trust law varies materially, and divorce also operates differently. The other major concern at present is the tax varying power under the Scotland Act 1997. The Scottish variable rate (SVR) can be 3 pence in the pound more or less than elsewhere and employees resident in Scotland will have a special tax code allocated them with an S prefix. Pension schemes would then have to deduct the extra tax (or charge a lower tax) and forward it to the Revenue. There are around 2.36 million Scottish taxpayers, of which 1.9 million are PAYE, not all of whom are liable to SVR. There are also 675,000 liable in the rest of the United Kingdom. Fortunately it is up to the individual to decide whether he or she is Scottish for these purposes or not, and not for the pension scheme or employer. There are, however, bound to be complexities, especially where pensions are paid, say, to a bank account of the pensioner, or where the pensions have been split on divorce.

Simplification

Pension arrangements are notoriously complicated in the United Kingdom. It is not surprising therefore that there have been calls for many years, for simplification of the system underlying the provision of pensions not only:

- by employees, because their retirement benefits are difficult to understand; but also
- by employers (and pension scheme managers), because the administration of pension schemes is complicated and expensive.

Much of this complexity has derived from a tax regime which has developed over more than 70 years. During that development period there have been changes both to the policies underlying the regime, and changes to the regime. As a consequence the regime that operates today is widely regarded as unwieldy and expensive to operate, and suffering from differing and sometimes conflicting objectives.

There may be practical alternatives to the current tax regime which can simplify the arrangements, yet protect the interests of all the interested parties including particularly:

- the members;
- the employers; and
- the Treasury.

Any alternatives suggested should enable the general public to understand better their pension arrangements and reduce costs for employers — resulting in savings for the community as a whole — without adding materially to Treasury costs (the main objection to previous suggested reforms).

Value of pensions in macroeconomic terms

Pension rights, and the funds guaranteeing their payment, are widely recognised not only as a personal asset of individuals, but as a significant national asset. This recognition is an international one, as it is appreciated that the size of the funds supporting the pension system represents a pool of capital of considerable value and one not available to many of the UK's trading competitors, as well as a protection against intergenerational conflict. About 10.5 million employees (50 percent of the workforce) are members of occupational schemes, and around 8 million employees and self-employed are covered (sometimes only modestly) by personal pensions. Over 7 million pensioners benefit currently from occupational schemes; funds of over £600 billion are involved with the system, with over £150 billion invested overseas.

These funded systems accordingly provide invisible export earnings (in contrast to the long-term demographic problems posed by unfunded systems in much of the rest of Europe); the financial services industry which has grown up around them is now generating overseas earnings, and the general financial and pensions expertise is one which is now widely employed by foreign jurisdictions.

Over the last half-century, accordingly, they have by most standards been regarded as a success (although not without their problems). It is clear, however, that this success is not guaranteed to continue into the future. The reasons for this uncertainty are complex and various; they include changing employment patterns less suited to collective provision (although this may be less real than perceived), a desire by employers to reduce apparent exposure to risk – and an increasingly complex legal regime, both fiscal and regulatory (with the costs that that entails). It is clearly not true that employers, for example, would be persuaded to dismantle schemes solely because of the need for compliance; but compliance costs are equally clearly a significant element in the decision-making as to future pension provision.

Should the state support private pension provision?

There is no automatic reason why the state should ensure fiscal neutrality to encourage the provision of private pension provision. Indeed there are occasional suggestions that the present tax neutrality for pension schemes should be abandoned. However, if no tax reliefs were available it would be cost-ineffective for employers in particular to provide pensions through prior funding; indeed a century ago most employer-based pension systems were pay-as-you-go. Other countries, most notably New Zealand, have experimented with attempts to discourage prior provision; the majority of jurisdictions, however, (including those who are now in course of introducing funded pension systems) have adopted or are adopting the taxation system which has operated in the United Kingdom since 1921, namely tax exemption on payments into the system, tax-exemption on investment income, and tax on the payment of benefits (known in the jargon as EET). This section is therefore written on the assumption that such a taxation system is the most appropriate and is likely to continue. It also assumes that the state has an interest in the encouragement of an environment for the provision of private pensions by avoiding the establishment or introduction of a penal or non-neutral tax regime.

The incidental advantages (and drawbacks) of private pension systems have been explored elsewhere; the advantages include a reduction in demand for state benefits, the creation of a pool of capital, and the establishment of a sense of personal responsibility.

Complexity of the fiscal regime

The acknowledged complexity of the UK's fiscal framework is not limited to the pensions system;

other areas of endeavour also frequently complain. And the drawbacks of a complex system are widely acknowledged. Accordingly, there have been several initiatives designed to simplify the system. The Prudential Corporation in 1996 issued a paper dedicated to an examination of the problem; its research group was chaired by Sir Michael Partridge, formerly the most senior civil servant at the DSS; it restricted its examination to tax issues. Its objective was, however, more limited than a subsequent NAPF inquiry.

Meanwhile, the Inland Revenue, for example, is already committed to simplifying the wording (although not the substance) of the fiscal legislation through its Tax Rewrite project. In relation to pensions in particular, the Prudential Corporation paper suggested that some parts of the system could be simplified by cutting back some of the technicalities; and the Occupational Pensions Joint Working Group (comprising many of the pensions bodies) has had continual liaison with the Inland Revenue on minor technical reforms.

But the sheer volume and complexity of the fiscal legislation otherwise shows little signs of easing; indeed the contrary seems the case. And in addition to the principal legislation there are statutory instruments, Inland Revenue Practice Notes arid Inland Revenue Updates, as well as press releases and other documents, some of which are highly complex.

The principal policy objective of any such arrangements is or should be to ensure that the fiscal neutrality applied to pension schemes is not taken undue advantage of by employees and employers. As mentioned, it is not always easy to discern such a coherent policy objective displayed in the mass of regulation. And the regulatory structure itself is not always easy to comply with because of its complexity, with the added danger that failure to comply may bring the whole system of regulation into disrepute. Finally, the system appears to apply only to a small minority of the population (conventionally stated to be about 1 percent) since the majority cannot afford to exceed the limits because of shortage of resources.

The question therefore is whether it is possible to design a more cost-effective system, untrammelled by historical impedimenta, which meets the sometimes conflicting needs and objectives of members, employers and government.

Simplification criteria

The tax treatment of pensions and pension schemes is a subject of great complexity. This results in part from the laudable desire of the Inland Revenue, when introducing changes, to avoid disturbing the accrued rights of those who are already scheme members. But the effect, as pointed out by the Pension Law Review Committee in its report "Pension Law Reform", is that every set of new rules creates its own distinct tax regime, so that different groups of members of one and the same scheme could be subjected to up to three different sets of rules. The complexity is exacerbated by the earnings cap and the requirement, where scheme benefits accrue at a rate faster than one-sixtieth of final salary for each year of service, to calculate for each scheme member the value of an individual's retained benefits over his or her working life. The sheer volume, and in many cases the obscurity, of regulations and practice notes with which those administering pension schemes and their advisers have to familiarise themselves is daunting.

Any alternatives to the present system need to meet a number of crucial criteria, including most crucially of all the absence of any cost to the Treasury. But it is clear that, in practice, a need for simplification is hardly in doubt, although most of the evidence seems empirical rather than rigorous. The complexity of the system, the costs (administrative, legal, actuarial) that emerge as a consequence, the fact that benefits are accordingly difficult to explain to members (although the excuse that the Revenue will not allow certain improvements is often a useful one), and the constraints on innovative product developments to meet the changing needs of modern employment practices are taken as a given fact by most observers of the system.

Any alternatives proposed need to take account of timing. The timing for reform of the taxation system seems propitious. There is a growing political consensus (by producers as well as consumers of legislation) against complexity. Even the Inland Revenue itself had been required to commission an expensive and long-term revision of the fiscal legislation, though only in form rather than substance. And the forthcoming stakeholder pensions proposed by an incoming administration demand a much simpler fiscal treatment than that available if they are ever to work as anticipated.

That time is not ripe, however, for a review of the other great area of complexity, social security law, particularly the regulatory environment post the 1995 Act. It is hardly a year since most of the legislation came into force and it is too early to judge its effectiveness or otherwise, although first indications are that there may an excess of zeal developing amongst the regulators, an occupational and inevitable hazard of the system, and that there may need to be a restructuring of some of the more profound drafting errors of the Act.

Kinds of simplification

Simplification covers not only substance but style. Style is already a matter for the Tax Rewrite project, with a £25 million budget.

However, of more interest is the content; it is the content that causes grief to the industry and to scheme members. And in looking at the content it seems sensible to look at systems which dealt not only with final salary systems but also defined contribution schemes; and, because of the increasing interplay between them, not only occupational but also personal schemes.

Tax structure

Before considering any general review, it is necessary to explore whether the existing tax schema is still appropriate. A great deal of work has been done on whether the EET system (exempt contributions, exempt build-up, and taxed benefits) is still appropriate in the United Kingdom. Experiments using other systems have been carried out elsewhere (most notably in New Zealand) and even in the United Kingdom the system is not entirely fiscally neutral, as the recent debates over the incidence of ACT indicate. But studies by the Institute of Fiscal Studies, and by the World Bank more recently have firmly indicated that EET is the preferred system. The World Bank studies also indicated that even where a scheme is compulsory (and therefore the incentive of tax relief no longer required) lack of tax relief (and consequent neutrality) would result in failure of the system, as it was perceived as unfair. It seems not unreasonable therefore to assume that the presently fiscally neutral system should continue; indeed there seems no other practicable alternative (which is not to say any government would not try to prejudice it).

Objectives of fiscal regulation

Fiscal regulation has two main objectives in an EET system:

- first, to limit the tax reliefs, where the reliefs are perceived as a tax break; and
- secondly, to limit abuse, or perceived abuse, of such reliefs as are available.

Over the years the fiscal authorities have imposed a series of controls in three main areas, although the controls have varied according to the nature of the scheme (ie whether they were defined contributions or defined benefit):

- contributions, including employers' contributions, employees' contributions, AVCs etc;
- benefits (the earnings cap, the two-thirds limit);
- investments (and surpluses).

Each of these controls has been introduced and

developed over time, often as a response to abuse of the reliefs or perceived abuse, or sometimes as a political statement. As the quotation from Professor Goode indicates, however, the current structure is complex. Does it need to be? And are there other ways of meeting the objectives of fiscal policy?

Are 1970/80 style fiscal controls necessary in 2000?

Sometimes lessons can be learned from a historical survey; the question which now arises some 75 years after the original fiscal neutrality was introduced by the 1921 legislation is whether the construct is now needed in its present form, especially as the factors which lead to the creation of the edifice may no longer exist.

Several external factors have changed, in particular:

- income tax rates have now fallen to such a level (and are unlikely to rise materially in the future) that the function of a pension scheme as a tax haven, prevalent especially in the mid-1970s when tax rates could on occasion reach 103 percent, no longer apply. Indeed, in some cases pensions are less attractive from a tax point of view than truly privileged tax breaks, such as ISAs and share options;
- there is an increasing understanding of cost-effectiveness in regulation; in other words, it may be appropriate to suffer a certain amount of abuse of the system where to control it perfectly would be not cost-effective, having regard to the administration and staffing costs. There is a certain amount of difficulty in cost-effectiveness, since the Revenue has now learnt the skill of designing systems which are cost-effective for it, but impose unquantifiable (though clearly expensive) compliance costs on the citizenry;
- the development of surpluses which the Revenue perceived as operating like a tax-haven has now gone into reverse; indeed more effort is now being devoted to recovery of surpluses than ensuring schemes stay

overfunded. This is another example of 1970's policies being carried over to the 1990s;

- the previous role of the Revenue as regulator and protector of the consumer has now been assumed by OPRA.

If there were to be a move to simplification, would that be regarded as a licence for anarchy? The Revenue and Treasury would clearly be concerned at possible losses of revenue. But others may also have concerns:

- legislators of any denomination find it difficult to let go once control has been gained and there will always be the odd case of default. This is now less likely with OPRA and the Pensions Act 1995, but it could be an issue;
- the press, unless it clearly understood the rationale, could feel uncomfortable with a reduced tax regime; it could be seen (as discussed below) as a fat cats' charter. The fact that it clearly would not be might be difficult to explain, even though any reform would in fact become thin cats' liberation;
- as mentioned, the existence of restrictions sometimes suits scheme managers in negotiations on pension benefits!

Revenue concerns

Revenue concerns are not a mere chimera, although it may be that their perception is not quite on all fours with reality. They include:

- whether pensions schemes are tax privileged or tax-neutral;
- whether there are short-term cash-flow costs to any simplification problem;
- whether simplification would lead to unacceptable inequity between higher and lower earners; in other words is simplification a subsidy by the poor of the rich? In particular:
  - are higher earners gaining more than is fair?
  - would pension funds be used as a tax-haven?

- would there be a cost to the Exchequer by individuals moving their income to marginal tax rates at retirement?
- would small self-administered schemes (SSAPS) abuse the position, especially in the light of the Roux experience, a case in which the Inland Revenue proved that a scheme was adjusted to escape tax?

Before examining these concerns, it may be constructive to look at the three main areas of control to see if they are necessary to achieve the purpose.

Controls

There are, as mentioned, controls on contributions, on benefits and on funding.

Controls on contributions in defined benefit schemes are actuarially determined by reference to a balance between funding and benefit levels. The question arises whether there are natural limits which could be used instead of arbitrary limits which have developed for historic reasons (largely related to benefit levels in the Civil Service) over the years.

Some observers consider that the natural limits would be sufficient in practice:

- the disposable income of most contributors is limited; it is reported (although the evidence is anecdotal) that only 1 percent of the population currently reach Revenue limits at present;
- the market forces operating on most employers would restrain excessive contributions, certainly in the larger schemes;
- the fact that benefits cannot (with an obvious exception) be taken in cash (unlike, say, ISAs) means that a pension is a very different animal from most other systems. A pension scheme is a deal between the individual and the state; in exchange for forswearing both current

consumption and future liquidity the state provides fiscal neutrality. A pension scheme is not therefore tax-advantaged but is neutral.

Controls on benefits are somewhat harder to understand as a form of Revenue protection. Since benefits are taxed, the more benefits, the more tax. There are no benefit limits in personal pensions, and the ones in defined benefit schemes are, as mentioned, arbitrary.

The question, as above, is whether in any event there are natural limits on benefits anyway. There might be natural limits in defined contribution schemes, since disposable income for most contributors will limit contributions and hence benefits. And in defined benefit schemes, since they must be employer-related, market forces will normally avoid excessive benefits, just as it limits (except in the City) excessive salaries.

Similar arguments apply to the earnings cap; why should there be an earnings cap on pensions, where there is no earnings cap on earnings (as there is, for example, in the United States)? If the state wished to impose a sumptuary law, the most effective way would be through limits on earnings, rather than on ancillary benefits related to earnings — where it causes huge complexities, with FURBS, GUFFSAPS, UURBS and the like quite properly being created at substantial expense in actuarial, administrative and legal time.

Finally, in relation to the super-rich, the Waddingham syndrome would apply. Adrian Waddingham, the distinguished actuary, in an article in *Pensions World* some time ago pointed out that a wealthy man was unlikely to allocate £1 million to his pension fund (after proper provision) where the income would show £60,000 since he could invest better elsewhere and not have to sacrifice the capital.

It is not wholly clear why, when tax rates are so low, there should still continue to be controls on funding, especially after the introduction of the minimum funding requirement. There are few employers or others who are enjoying surpluses who are not exploring the question of repatriation of surpluses. The pension fund as tax haven may no longer exist; and the tax charge, which causes so much additional work on valuations and tax planning is an inconvenience which raises relatively little money for the state, most of which anyway would be taxable through company profits. The funding restrictions again may be a response to the excesses of the 1980s and the tax levels of the 1970s; whether they are of significant material benefit today may be open to question.

Principle of controls

It is clear that anarchy is no way to run a railway. On the other hand, many of the controls in place today may be a hangover from very different economic arid commercial conditions. Each of the current controls may need reassessment, with justification on pragmatic grounds; and perhaps considering targeted and simple controls. Any control framework would need to be very much simpler than that at present in force, with substantial savings (if they operate) for both the community and the government. Such controls could replicate those available abroad, such as a requirement that all benefits (subject to a cap on lump sums) be paid in pension form, that any investment should not permit a present user, and that schemes continue to be approved (to ensure proper payment of benefits). This would allow the present controls on retirement ages, on retained benefits, on headroom calculations and the rest of the paraphernalia to be consigned to the flames.

The objectives of control would be to ensure that there is improved understanding by all parties, easier policing, better communication with members, reduced compliance costs, higher take-up by members, reduced social security spending and, not least, increased competitiveness in Europe. It is becoming increasingly clear that unless UK pension systems are rendered more competitive from a compliance and fiscal point of view, they will lose out to pension arrangements established by multinationals and others in those Member States with simpler rules.

With the latest document issued by the NAPF, the increasing consensus of both legislators and consumers, the fresh approaches being adopted by the Revenue and the Treasury, and the need to redraft the fiscal system to meet the needs of the incipient stakeholder pensions, the time has never been better to review the present fiscal regime affecting UK pensions. It is likely that reforms will be introduced, and that they will involve substantial reductions in the controls on contributions, funding and benefits. The advantages would include reduced compliance and administration costs, improved pensions take-up, and a more competitive EU position.

- *Making Pensions Easy*, NAPF, April 1998
- Richard Baron, "Tax relief for pensions", Institute of Directors, 0171-451 3212, June 1998
- Consumer Misunderstanding on Pensions, a study by the Association of Unit Trusts and Investment Funds, 0171-831 0898, June 1998.

SSASs

SSASs or small self-administered schemes are loathed by insurers because they divert investments away from their control and by the mainstream industry because they are seen as tax devices rather than true pension schemes. In fact the vast majority of SSASs are invested mostly in cash, and are expertly managed. However, fresh regulations in 1998 were intended to tighten up control by the Inland Revenue who have always been suspicious of such schemes. Nowadays a SSAS is a scheme with fewer than 12 members, holds assets which are not insurance policies and where any scheme member is "connected" with any member, trustee or employer in relation to the scheme. There are strict rules on what such schemes can invest in, what benefits they can pay, and how they are funded.

Although SSASs have to comply with strict revenue rules and are required to have a special trustee, known as a pensioneer trustee, there are significant advantages to having a SSAS compared to an insured scheme or a self-administered personal pension.

Permitted investments

Unlike other pension schemes, SSASs are not subject to the same restrictions on investment in the sponsoring company. This means that SSASs can:

- purchase shares of the principal employer or its holding company;
- make loans to the principal employer; and
- acquire commercial premises to be let to the principal employer.

Pensioneer trustee

In return for this flexibility SSASs are required to have a pensioneer trustee – recognised by the Inland Revenue as having pensions expertise – whose role is to provide guidance and ensure compliance with the Revenue's rules. In practice, pensioneer trustees are pension professionals who market SSASs to family-owned companies.

Purchase of shares in the principal employee

A SSAS may purchase company shares subject to a limit of 30 percent of the issued share capital. In the early years of a SSAS no more than 25 percent of the value of the fund can be invested in this way rising to 50 percent after two years, but in both cases after including in this limit the value of any loans made to the employer.

An investment in shares must be reported to the Pension Schemes Office (PSO) within 90 days and supported by a professional share valuation to demonstrate that the acquisition has been at a fair market value.

Purchase of commercial property

This is often seen as one of the main advantages of a SSAS as providing not only a solid tax free investment return for the scheme, but also allowing the company to obtain tax relief on its rental payments which roll-up tax free in the SSAS. Again, property transactions are closely regulated and subject to reporting requirements. If the property is acquired from the principal employer a professional valuation which can be justified to the District Valuer is necessary as the Revenue will instruct the District Valuer's office to confirm that the transaction has been carried out at arms length. Transactions at an undervalue/overvalue may lead to loss of approval. Similarly, the lease between the SSAS and the employer has to be on commercial terms. The PSO regard commercial property as a long term investment and will not grant approval to property acquisition where they believe it inappropriate – such as when all of the scheme members are approaching retirement.

Borrowing

SSASs like other self-administered schemes are permitted to borrow to acquire investments, but in the case of a SSAS borrowing is limited to the greater of 45 percent of the market value of the scheme's assets and three times the average employer contribution in the preceding three years. Special rules apply where the scheme has been established for less than this period. Again, a SSASs borrowings have to be reported to the PSO within 90 days.

Loans

Many SSASs have provided unsecured loans to the employing company. The PSO require a commercial rate of interest (at least 3 percent above base rate) and immediate repayment if the capital is needed to pay pensions to members. Similar limits to those mentioned in respect of share purchase apply to the amount that can be loaned to the employer.

Prohibition on dealings with scheme members

Since 1991, SSASs have not been able to buy or sell permitted investments to or from scheme members or any person or company "connected" with them. These regulations do not prevent member dealing in respect of assets (usually commercial property) acquired prior to 1991 but the Revenue will look closely to ensure that any transaction is carried out at market value and will not hesitate to disapprove a SSAS if a property is sold at an undervalue.

Annuity deferral

SSASs were allowed to delay annuity purchase for up to five years following retirement before the introduction of annuity deferral. Since 1994, SSASs have been permitted to delay annuity purchase until the member's 75th birthday, subject to actuarial reviews to check that the level of pension can be maintained. Where a member's annuity purchase has been deferred the value of the underlying assets underpinning the pension in payment is disregarded for the purpose of calculating the maximum amounts which the scheme may borrow or invest in the company's shares.

Deliberate loss of tax approval

In recent years a small but significant practice of deliberately losing scheme approval has developed, which the Revenue, understandably, has been quick to counter. A 40 percent tax charge is levied on loss of approval and any distribution of scheme capital will trigger a further tax charge as the special rules applying to Funded Unapproved Retirement Benefit Schemes are disapplied in relation to SSASs which have been disapproved. More recently wider powers have been introduced to enable the Revenue to collect the tax charge from scheme members, particularly where the scheme assets have been transferred abroad leaving the sponsoring employer as a "shell" with no assets to pay the tax charge.

Pensions Act 1995

SSASs are exempt from the majority of the Pensions Act's Regulations, provided all the members are trustees and they make their decisions unanimously. There is some inconsistency in the wording of the exemptions which in some cases apply only if member trustees alone can make the appropriate decision -the pensioneer trustee being ignored for these purposes. This means that for single member schemes if an additional independent trustee is desired the "penalty" is compliance with some of the Pensions Act's requirements (eg money-purchase contribution schedule and appointment of auditor) from which other SSASs are exempt provided all decisions are made by the member trustees unanimously.

Conclusion

In many cases a SSAS is by far the most appropriate method of pension provision for owner controllers because of the greater investment flexibility and tax planning opportunities afforded to the sponsoring company. The fact that the charges associated with a SSAS are explicit and not "lost" within an insurer's pricing structure makes a SSAS a very attractive proposition for owner controllers who also wish to retain control over the way in which they provide for their retirement.

- Retirement Benefits Schemes (Restriction on Discretion to Approve) (Small Self-administered Schemes) (Amendment) Regulations 1998, SI 1998 No 728; Retirement Benefits Schemes (Restriction on Discretion to Approve) (Excepted Provisions) Regulations 1998, SI 1998 No 729

- The Association of Pensioneer Trustees operates as a trade association of promoters of SSASs and publishes a technical newsletter

- *R* v *Inland Revenue* ex p *Roux Waterside Inn* [1997] PLR 123.

Ian Davies, *Cardiff*

SIPPs

SIPPs or Self-Invested Personal Pensions have been the success story of the pensions movement in the 1990s. They are poised for further growth as the move towards disintermediated Group Personal Pensions (GPPs) (*qv*) increases, where the costs of administration and investment are charged as fees rather than concealed as commissions and overheads.

SIPPs are particularly attractive to the higher-paid professional where the normal insurance company overheads on higher contributions are disproprotionate. They also give the opportunity to invest in a wide range of investments other than (and as well as) insurance products. In recent years there has been a great interest in property as an investment, although there are technical concerns.

The Revenue rules outlining what may and may not be done in a SIPP are set out in memorandum 101, still extant despite it having been issued in 1989, and in particular constrain the kind of property investments. Residential property is outlawed, with some minor exceptions, and property may not be bought from connected parties, or anyone connected with them in the last three years.

Property

One of the major advantages of SIPPs is the opportunity to invest in property. Unlike in a SASS, the property is pooled with other members of the SIPP, which in an insured arrangement could be very many. It is critical therefore that not only are the Revenue rules complied with, but also that other SIPP members are not affected by a diminution in the value of the property. Unlike many other assets, property can have a negative value and thus diminish the value of other member's SIPPs.

Differences with SSASs

Contributions to SIPPs are limited by the restrictions on contributions that the self-employed can make. In practice most SIPPs are established by transfers from other schemes, with the average first contribution including transfers of around £60,000.

- John Moret, "Bricks and mortar investment guide", *Investment Week*, 25 May 1998.

Stakeholder pensions

At present few are sure just what stakeholder pensions are. They are intended to cope with the reduction in the scope of the state pension (*qv*) and to cope with the needs of persons not covered by SERPS, eg housewives and carers whose needs were intended to the dealt with by the "citizens pensions" which no longer seems to be mentioned. The gaps between the richer and poorer pensioners also appears to be widening.

- Pension Provision Group, We all need pensions: the prospects for pension provision ("The Ross Report") Stationery Office, 1998, ISBN 001-762607 4 £25. Brief: "To determine the current levels of pension provision in the UK and likely future trends..."

State pension

The basic state pension is linked to prices rather than wages, and is therefore reducing in value year by year. In 1995/96 26.0 million people gained a qualifying year for the basic state retirement pension; around 5.3 million received a Home Responsibilities credit. Of the 26 million, 10.2 million are women (up from 5.9 million in 1978/79).

- Department of Social Security, Analytical Services Division, *Contributions and Qualifying Years for Retirement Pension 1995/96*, June 1998, 2 vols (David Ferguson 0191-225 7094).

Surplus

Few areas give rise to heated legal debate as much as on the question of surpluses. There is clearly a deep misunderstanding about their nature in final salary balance of cost schemes, and the drafting of scheme provisions is sometimes examined by the courts with meticulous care when they were clearly intended not to have such interpretations lavished on them. It does not help that the word surplus is used so cavalierly; if the actuarial profession had used "actuarial reserves" or some similar phrase, it would have avoided a great deal of misunderstanding which continues to this day.

Leading cases include *Air Products Canada* v *Schmidt* [1995] PLR 75 (Canada); *British Coal Corporation* v *British Coal Staff Superannuation Scheme Trustees* [1995] 1 All ER 912; [1993] PLR 303; *Re Courage Group's Pension Schemes* [1987] 1 WLR 495; *Hillsdown Holdings* v *Pensions Ombudsman* [1997] 1 All ER 862; *Imperial Group Pension Trust* v *Imperial Tobacco* [1991] 1 WLR 589; *National Grid* v *Laws* [1997] PLR 157; *Lock* v *Westpac Banking Corporation* [1991] PLR 167; *Mettoy Pension Trustees* v *Evans* [1990] 1 WLR 1587; *Packwood* v *British Airways* [1995] PLR 189; *Thrells* v *Lomas* [1993] 1 WLR 456; *UEB Industries* v *Brabant* [1991] PLR 109; *Edge* v *Pensions Ombudsman* [1998] PLR 15; *Stannard* v *Fisons Pension Trust* [1991] PLR 225; *Re William Makin & Son* [1992] PLR 177.

- Geoffrey Topham, "Trustees' duties in relation to surplus", paper to Ark Conferences, June 1998, 3 Stone Buildings Lincoln's Inn, 0171-242 4937.

Trustees

Following the introduction of member-nominated trustees in the Pensions Act 1995, there has been concern about their liability. There are several guides to their training and duties, and there is now a defence union, OPDU (*qv*) dedicated to their protection. Qualifications are issued by the PMI and other organisations.

Trustee defence

A lot has been written on the duties and potential liabilities of pension scheme trustees in the light of the Pensions Act 1995. A new trustee might be forgiven for viewing the appointment as something of a poisoned chalice. The truth is somewhat different, and on closer examination the "defences" available to trustees are perhaps greater than the fledgling trustee might expect. If a trustee acts prudently and takes professional advice where appropriate, the question of liability and defence should not arise. Where it does, the scheme's exoneration and indemnity provisions should provide a pretty solid line of defence, with an application to the courts, or insurance policies being an effective, if expensive, second line of defence.

Indemnity clauses

A well-drawn trust deed will contain an indemnity for trustees so that in cases where they have been found liable they are individually indemnified out of the scheme's assets or by the employer. So, if a successful claim is brought against the trustees, for example, for not paying the correct amount of pension, the cost of putting things right is met by the fund or if it has insufficient assets by the employer. Clearly an indemnity from an employer is only as good as its ability to pay, and is of no use if the employer goes out of business. Indemnities will not cover liability arising from an improper act and under section 31 of the Pensions Act and indemnity from the fund is ineffective against a fine imposed by statute. Some older trust deeds might not contain an indemnity clause, but even if this is the case there is a limited indemnity available to trustees under section 31 of the Trustee Act 1925 (it does not for example cover paying benefits to the wrong person).

Exoneration clauses

These clauses are designed to prevent liability arising in the first place unless the trustee has been dishonest. Many pension deeds contain both an exoneration clause and an indemnity provision. Exoneration clauses have been tested in the courts recently and found effective. In *Armitage* v *Nurse* (1997) the Court of Appeal found that the wording of an exoneration clause in a private trust deed which excluded the trustees from liability for loss or damage "unless such loss or damage shall be caused by his own actual fraud" to be fully effective and that the words "actual fraud" should be interpreted by giving them their normal meaning and not extended to mean "constructive" or "equitable" fraud. The judge went on to add that even if trustees had deliberately committed a breach of trust, but did so in good faith believing they were acting in the beneficiary's best interests, there could be no fraud on their part.

Section 33 of the Pensions Act 1995

This section has not yet been the subject of litigation but prevents exclusion of liability for loss arising from the trustees' failure to invest the scheme funds properly – or in practice to monitor correctly their investment manager. Some commentators have suggested this means that the cost of insuring trustee liability for investment losses cannot be met from the fund and that schemes' exoneration and indemnity provisions will be ineffective against such claims. While it is likely that an exoneration clause and indemnity from the fund could be successfully attacked under this section, an indemnity from a solvent employer would remain effective and the case prohibiting the fund's payment of insurance premiums against risks including investment losses has not been fully made.

Insurance

The early policies available to trustees were of such poor value that after the exclusions had been stripped out it was difficult to see what actual cover was provided in return for the premium. Fortunately the position has begun to change and insurance may in certain circumstances be a valid consideration for trustees. More recently new products have been developed such as the Occupational Pensions Defence Union (OPDU). This was established by Thomas Miller & Co Ltd in conjunction with their professional liability insurance arm. Unlike traditional policies, OPDU provides an advisory service to help prevent disputes turning into claims as well as the more usual scheme insurance and run off cover for retired trustees.

Applications to the court

Trustees faced with litigation are permitted to apply to the court for a direction that no matter what the outcome their costs will be met by the fund. More recently this has been reflected by the growing number of cases in which claimants have been successful in obtaining pre-emptive orders for their costs in order to allow them to bring claims against trustees. This is a growing area of the law reflecting the commercial nature of pension trusts.

Fees of independent trustees

Independent trustees are often appointed on insolvency of the employer or on wind-up of a scheme. There has been concern in recent years about the fees and expenses run up by such trustees, who often feel they need to over-engineer their advice to protect themselves. Court decisions in recent years and advice from OPRA is that trustees should be pragmatic in such cases and "take a view" rather than be excessively cautious.

Conclusion

There are perhaps more defences available to trustees than prospective candidates for the post may be led to believe. In the vast majority of cases trustees acting prudently, honestly and after taking professional advice will not need to look in depth at the exoneration and indemnity provisions of their trust deeds. If they do need to do so they will find them generally effective unless they have been guilty of fraud. Insurance can play a role, but should be purchased after taking appropriate professional advice.

- OPRA, *Selecting Trustees*, March 1997, 01273 627600
- OPRA, *A Guide for Pension Scheme Trustees*, 01273 637600

- Robin Ellison, *The Pension Trustees Handbook*, Thorogood, 0171-824 8257, £25
- OPRA, Guidance to trustees appointed by OPRA, Bulletin No 3, May 1998 Appendix 2, sets down a code of practice for OPRA appointed trustees
- Karen Blunt, Mark Winterbotham & Robert Williams, The Role of Pension Scheme Trustees, DSS Research Report No 81, July 1989, ISBN 1-84123-001-4, £28.

Ian Davies, *Cardiff*

TUPE

See also Cases: review.

On take-overs, employees' employment rights are protected by amongst other things the provisions of the Transfer of Undertakings Regulations. The Regulations are made under the requirements of the European Union Acquired Rights Directive. The Directive and the Regulations currently exclude pension rights from protection (but oddly probably not personal pensions provided or supported by the employer). The European Commission is proposing to remove the current exemption for pensions as is the Department of Trade and Industry, but there are significant practical problems (which is why the exemption was there in the first place.) However, changes are not expected for some time yet.

- Department of Trade and Industry, Press release P/98/430, New Clear Rules Assure Employees' Transfer Rights, 4 June 1998
- Eversheds Technical Note 1998/04, "Are GPPs covered by TUPE?"

Underwriting commissions

One of the ways in which pension funds, especially the larger ones, can increase their returns is by engaging in sub-underwriting for investment banks. The procedure is that the pension fund, usually through their fund managers, agree to buy some new shares of a company being issued to raise new capital. The Inland Revenue in recent years has argued that such activity is a trade and not an investment, and therefore taxable. It lost the first main case at the end of 1997, but it is expected that the battle will continue, especially if the Revenue can appeal or find other cases which differ on the facts. In the 1997 *British Telecom* case the Special Commissioners held that sub-underwriting "formed an integral part of the investment process and took its colour therefrom" because the pension scheme saw the whole process of the underwriting of issues as a part of the capital raising process and a way of maintaining the weighting of their holdings in an essentially index-tracking portfolio. They had not set out to generate commissions as such.

David Wainman, *London*

- *British Telecom Pension Scheme* v *Clarke* [1998] PLR 87.

VAT

The general consensus is that VAT is payable on administration costs but not on investment services costs; in practice many funds bundle the two together. It is one of the advantages of corporate trustees that it can be made part of group VAT registration for the purposes of recovering otherwise unrecoverable VAT. There is a useful though partisan booklet issued by Customs and Excise on VAT and most trustee fees which bear VAT are now recoverable. A consultation document (Restriction of VAT Groups to Fully Taxable Corporate Bodies, June 1998) suggests that the rules may be changed to exclude pension trustee companies from such groups, in which case, if implemented, VAT planning may need to be revised.

Whistleblowing

The Public Interest Disclosure Act 1998 expands whistleblowing as a general concept outside the requirements of pension funds alone. Under the Pensions Act 1995 only actuaries and whistleblowers have the obligation to whistleblow, although others may do so to OPRA. Most customer agreements with actuaries and accountants grant them authority to do so, and provide that trustees and employers are under an obligation to provide information. The Public Interest Disclosure Act 1998 merely awards compensation of up to £47,000 from an employer to an employee who is victimised for making a disclosure in certain areas, such as where he has a reasonable belief that a criminal offence has been committed or is likely to be committed. There is an obligation to sort things out with the employer first.

Winding-up

Winding-up is proving an intractable problem; not only are there restrictions under section 67 of the Pensions Act 1995 on amending the deed and rules which used to be common practice on a wind-up, but there are problems on paying state scheme premiums in relation to contracted-out rights back to the state, or receiving GMP valuations from the Contributions Agency because of difficulties in the national insurance computer. There are also concerns about the costs of wind-up, especially where trustees feel unable to take commercial decisions and insist on strict construction of the rules, which can involve disproportionate expense.

- Karen Bunt, David Howells & Mark Winterbotham, *Experiences of Occupational Pension Scheme Wind-up*, Stationery Office, April 1998, ISBN 0-11-762584-1, £27

- For legislation, see Pensions Act 1995 section 74 (which allows trustees to discharge the scheme's liabilities for pensions and other benefits which may not be allowed for in the rules); Occupational Pension Schemes (Winding-up) Regulations 1996, SI 1996 No 3126 and the Occupational Pension Schemes (Disclosure of Information) Regulations 1996, SI 1996 No 1655. There are also Institute of Actuary guidelines and statutory instruments dealing with deficiencies on winding-up, and possible claims against the Pensions Compensation Board where a deficiency is due to fraud.

Dates

1999

March

11	PMI Spring Conference
24–26	NAPF Investment Conference, Eastbourne

April

2	Good Friday
5	Easter Monday

May

3	May Day
13	PMI Annual Dinner
20–21	NAPF Annual Conference
31	Spring Bank Holiday

August

30	Late Summer Bank Holiday

October

7	PMI Autumn Conference

November

6	SPC Annual Conference
18	NAPF Autumn Conference, London
tbc	APL Annual Conference
tbc	Institute of Actuaries Annual Conference

December

27	Christmas Bank Holiday
28	Boxing Day Bank Holiday

2000

March

15–17	NAPF Investment Conference, Eastbourne

May

11–12	NAPF Annual Conference, Glasgow

November

23	NAPF Autumn Conference, London

Publications

Professional advisers (and the very large pension funds) have access to the *Perspective* (Pendragon 0171-393 7500) service of pensions information, with full text legislation, law reports, parliamentary debates, government publications and news updated daily and cross-referenced to within an inch of its life. But it may be a little like overkill for finance directors, and there is always a need for more specialist tomes.

Accounting

The impact of SSAP 24, the standard set by the accountancy profession for the disclosure of pensions obligations in the accounts of companies, has concentrated the minds of many companies on the pensions issue.

One of the most useful guides is Amyas Mascarenhas & Mary-Anne McIntyre (Deloitte & Touche), *Accounts & Audit of Pension Schemes* Butterworths, 1997, 3rd ed, 240pp, ISBN 0-406-05198-4, £55

Review of major practical problems of SSAP 24 (FRAG 10/92, 1992, ICAEW, gratis)

For local authorities, see *Statement on the Application of SSAP 24 Accounting for Pension Costs*, CIPFA, 1992, £15

Accounting for Overseas Investments by UK Pension Funds, NAPF Notes on Pensions with PRAG, No 12, £4

Pension Schemes Annual Reports, NAPF, 1987, No 17, £7.50

Accounting for Insurance Policies in Pension Schemes, NAPF, 1988, No 18, £7

Administration

Pension fund managers frequently face problems when dealing with their employers and their administrators. Improving communications is the subject of a study by the Pensions Research Accountants Group: Practical Problems at the Pension Fund/Company Interface: Pensions Information Flow – the Company Link, PRAG, 1992, A4, 15pp, free from IDS 0171-250 3434,

Robert Leach, *Financial Times Guide to Your Company Pension,* Financial Times Business Information, September 1990, 212 pp, ISBN 185334-045-6, £9.50

D Blake, *Issues in Pension Funding,* Routledge, 1992

Evans & Ward, *Pensions – Your Way through the Maze*, ICAEW, 3rd ed, £24.95

Tolley's *Pensions Administration*, looseleaf, 0181-686 9141, £125

Advice to members

Few trustees and managers give advice unless they are authorised; but for those that do try:

Butterworths Tax and Financial Planning Through Pensions, ed Peter Smith, Butterworths, 1992, 2nd ed, 238pp, ISBN 0-406-00580-X, £37.50

For handing out to pensioners, we suggest *Your Rights 1997-98*, Age Concern, £2.50, less in bulk

Myles MacCormack, *Pension Planning* is designed as a guide for solicitors who fancy themselves as personal pensions salesmen; nonetheless it is a handy trot through basic pensions arrangements, Law Society Publications, A5 pb, 152pp, £11.95

You and Your Pension, 1990, Which?, Hodder & Stoughton, ISBN 0340-503734, £8.95

Communication

A useful, simple and well-written guide, setting out sample booklets and newsletters is Sue Ward, *Pensions: Promoting and Communicating Your*

Scheme, the Industrial Society Press, 1990, ISBN 0-85290-472-X, £16.95

Employers

Preparing for Retirement: the Employer's Guide, a Pre-retirement Guide for Employers, sponsored by Mercer Fraser, Age Concern, 1992, £12.95

European and international

A handy summary of the EC law relating to pension schemes is set out in *EC Pensions Law* (written by (now former) members of Nicholson Graham & Jones, Chancery Law Publishing, 350pp, looseleaf, ISBN 85630-014-5, £115, sadly not updated for several years

Investments

Daniel Broby, *The Changing Face of European Fund Management*, FT Financial Publishing, 0171-896 2698, March 1997, 160pp, ISBN 1-85334-743-4, £395

Europe

Debbie Harrison, *Pension Provision and Fund Management in Europe,* FT Financial Publishing, 0171-896 2698, February 1997, ISBN 1-85334-687-X, £420

Always as up to date as these things can be, *International Benefit Guidelines 1998,* Mercers, 01372 379044, 21st ed, 333pp, 63 countries, free

The 1998 Guide to Pensions and Labour Law in Europe (with Japan and the USA), Sedgwick Noble Lowndes, 1998, ISBN 0-9521403-0-6, £40

Robin Ellison, *Pensions: Europe and Equality* (a pragmatic guide) Sweet & Maxwell, September 1995, 2nd ed, ISBN 075200 199X, £102.95

Debbie Harrison, *Pension Provision in the EC: Opportunities for the Private Sector in the Single Market*, Financial Times Management Reports, 1994, 2nd ed ISBN 1 85334 216 5, £293

Debbie Harrison, *Global pension strategies*, covers private pension solutions in developed and emerging economies; useful for multinationals, FT Finance, 0171-896 2294, April 1998, ISBN 85334 9143, £650

European Pensions Report 1994, a statistical report with the opinions of 180 of the largest European pension funds in 16 countries in relation to investment strategies and intentions, Global Research, US$730

European Pension Fund Managers Guide, Mercers, 0171-222 9121, Vol I, 1998, Vol II, 1997, £550 Vol I, £500 Vol II, £900 the two volumes. Volume I looks at European pension fund markets in 14 countries and is published annually; Volume II gives a profile on each investment manager operating within the markets.

For Ireland, see *Exempt Managed Funds Survey,* Irish Pensions Trust, 00353 1604 8100, free

For expatriate practice, see 1997-98 *Worldwide Survey of International Assignment Policies and Practices,* Organisation Resources Counselors Inc, 001 1212 852 0308, US$500

David Callund (ed), *Managing International Benefits* could form the basis of a primer in international benefits, Longmans, December 1994, ISBN 075200 0020, £95

Rather disorganised, but invaluable to those who need to know is *IBIS Online* available through the internet at a fee of £840 per annum; it gives information mostly of use to international benefit consultants reproducing technical information produced by the Chicago-based IBIS service. IBIS editorial Office, 250 S Wacker Drive, Chicago, Illinois, 60606, USA, 001-312 993 7900

China

China Personnel Practice: Benefits and Employment Terms, The Wyatt Company (HK) Ltd 1993/94, US$500

Investment

A simple guide is Colin Lever & David Hager, *Pension Fund Investment*, Butterworths, 1989, ISBN 0-406-50052

A more technical approach to the law of investments is set out in John Quarrell, *Law of Pension Fund Investment*, Butterworths, 1990, ISBN 0-406-67819-7, £65

Socially Responsible Investment: The Financial Impact of Screened Investment in the 1990's, Financial Times Management Reports, May 1991, ISBN 1 85334 143 6, £210

The Guide to Investment Managers Across Europe, William M Mercer Fraser, seems to be the only guide of its kind but it is costly. It summarises the services of 120 firms in the UK and in 10 other countries, £550 to trustees

Investment Management: A Guide for Trustees, NAPF Notes on Pensions No 20, 1992 ed, ISBN 0-905796-51-938p, £4.00 is a perfect "noddy" guide

Property Investment and Pension Funds, PRAG, 1987, is a technical analysis of some of the accounting and reporting problems, £85

D Kehrer, *Pension Plan Investor*, McGraw-Hill, 1991, ISBN 0077-074882, £29.95 designed for the US reader

Creative Tension, NAPF, discusses the role that pension funds should play as investors, £10

Pension Plan Investments: Confronting Today's Legal Issues, US, Practising Law Institute, 1992, $75, with audiocassette program, add $175

Bevis Longstreth, *Modern Investment Management and the Prudent Man Rule*, Oxford University Press, 1986, ISBN 0-19-504196-8 is still the best there is

Performance measurement

Investment Performance Measurement for UK Pension Funds, PRAG, 1989, £12.50

Committee of Enquiry Report into Investment Performance Measurement, NAPF, £40

Law

Textbooks

There is one major textbook, Robin Ellison, *Pensions Law and Practice,* Sweet & Maxwell, looseleaf, ISBN 0-85121-306-5, £285. Well-printed, three volumes, and looks impressive on the bookshelf though may be a little intimidating for everyday use. Major funds and advisers will find it essential.

Less comprehensive, though useful on aspects of trust law, and with an immense chapter on contracting-out, is Inglis-Jones, *The Law of Occupational Pensions*, Sweet & Maxwell, looseleaf, £180, annual service

Simmons and Simmons, *Pensions: The New Regime,* Sweet & Maxwell, 1998, ISBN 0421 619 309 288pp A4, looks at the impact of the Pensions Act 1995 and the regulations

Another guide is Nabarro Nathanson, *UK Pensions Law*, Butterworths, 1997, 390pp, ISBN 0-406 899207, £42

Very handy as a basic guide is Jonathan Seres, *Pensions: A Practical Guide*, Sweet & Maxwell, 1997, 4th ed, ISBN 075200 2465, £53

Trust Deed and Rules Checklist, NAPF, No 16, £4

Xenia Frostick has written *Pensions Law in Plain English,* in two volumes (!), the first dealing with the Pension Schemes Act 1993 and the second with the Pensions Act 1995, Palladian Law Publishing, November 1998, ISBN 1-902558 03 0,/ 1 902558 04 9, 176pp, £38

Disputes

Untested is Hammond Suddards, *Pension Disputes: Prevention and Resolution,* Jordans, 0117-923 0600, March 1998, ISBN 0-85308 413 0

Standard, but a little dated is Robin Ellison's, *Pensions Disputes: Law, Practice and Reform*, Sweet & Maxwell, May 1995, ISBN 075200 2368

For those with Ombudsman problems, Mark Grant, *The Pensions Ombudsman,* Sweet & Maxwell, July 1998, ISBN 075200 6037, £125

Equity and trusts

The standard book is Underhill & Hayton, *Law Relating to Trusts and Trustees*, Butterworths, 1987,14th ed, ISBN 0-406-4-593-X, £147 inc 1992 supp. None of the other books treats trusts as they need to be treated for pensions.

A rather tendentious consideration of the law is in Richard Nobles, *Pensions Empoyment and the Law,* Oxford Monographs on Labour Law, Clarendon Press, 1993, ISBN 0-19-825448-2, £35

Law reports

The standard law reports series are *Pensions Law Reports,* IDS 250 3434, £295 per annum

Also sometimes used are *Occupational Pensions Law Reports*, Eclipse, in a format which closely follows that of PLR; there have been delays recently in issuing reports, £265 per annum

Surpluses

Philip Bennett, *Pension Fund Surpluses*, Longmans, December 1993, 2nd ed, ISBN 075200 0128, £75

Mergers and acquisitions

Andrew White & Jonathan Punter, *Pensions Issues in Mergers and Acquisitions*, Sweet & Maxwell, 1996, 2nd ed, ISBN 0752002937, £125

An American approach is set out in Gordon Clark, *Pensions and Corporate Restructuring in American Industry*, John Hopkins University Press, 1993, ISBN 0-8018-4523-8, £33

Legislation

The amount of raw pensions law has increased over the last 20 years from about 40 pages to about 2,500 pages. It is all reproduced, more or less accurately in *Butterworths Pensions Legislation,* looseleaf, £250 approx

More useful and better value is the one-volume compendium issued every year by Pendragon, Robin Ellison (ed), *The Pensions Practice*, Pendragon, 0171-393 7500, 1997, ISBN 1-901436 01-2, around £60, and cheaper from NAPF

Pensions Handbook, Tolleys, October 1994, 2nd ed, ISBN 0-85459 916-9, is pre-1995 Act and now rather dated, but a good summary in its time, £41.95

Reform

The Goode Report, *Pension Law Reform*, is a classic of its kind – easy reading and even now a brilliant survey of the legal structure of schemes; what would he say if he could see what effect his suggestions have had on the movement? Cm 2342-I, HMSO, September 1993, £50 (research volume supplied separately)

Divorce

By the time this Handbook is out, the Pensions Sharing Act 1999 should have been passed, and is expected to be in force by April 2000.

Robin Ellison & Maggie Rae, *Family Breakdown and Pensions* (for the IFA and divorce practitioner), Butterworths, 1997, ISBN 0-406 03766 3, £35

The DSS issued the background guidance on pensions sharing as *Pensions Sharing on Divorce,* June 1998, 2 vols, free, no reference numbers

Winding-up

Karen Hunt, David Howells, & Mark Winterbotham, "Experiences of Occupational Pension Scheme Wind-up", Department of Social Security Social Security Research Series Report No 75, Stationery Office, April 1998, ISBN 0-11-762584-1, £27

The pension system

There are innumerable guides to the pensions system. One of the more practical though a little technical is Tony Reardon, *Allied Dunbar Pensions Handbook*, Pitman Publishing, 1997, 6th ed, ISBN 0-273 62506 3, £24.99

Most of the advisers will refer from time to time to Bob Escolme and others, *Hosking's Pension Schemes and Retirement Benefits*, Sweet & Maxwell, 1991, 6th ed, ISBN 0-421-41350-6, £50 which is designed for company secretaries and finance directors

More general is Bacon & Woodrow, *Pension Scheme Planning,* Butterworths, 1989, ISBN 0-406-50227-7, as is

Pension Increases: A Research paper on the Costs, Risks and Desirability of Alternative Strategies for Increasing Occupational Pensions During Retirement, NAPF, 1992, free, £5 handling charge

Pensions in Practice 1998/99 (annual) IDS, 0171-250 3434 is a useful and compact guide, £81

Industry

Matthew Craig, *The Future of UK Occupational Pensions*, FT Finance, November 1997, ISBN 1-85334-982-8, £450. A survey-based report

Comparatives

There is no shortage on works on which is the best insurance policy; unfortunately none of them will tell you which will be the best policy in 25 years' time. Figures are published monthly in *Money Management*, and you can buy Debbie Harrison, *Additional Voluntary Contributions 1998*, annual, Financial Times Business Information, ISBN 1-85334-053-7, which gives lists of companies and the policies they offer, £43

John Sheffield, *Executives and Directors and Top up Pensions 1998,* annual, Financial Times Finance, ISBN 1-85334-849 X, £65

With all the jargon about, *Pensions Terminology* is a handy guide. The latest edition has another 112 definitions, PRAG, Pensions Management Institute, 1992, 4th ed, ISBN 0-946242 74 7, £7

Maurice Oldfield, *Tolley's Understanding Occupational Pension Schemes*, Tolley, April 1994, 5th ed, 162pp, ISBN 1-851900878-2, £19.95

The Pensions Factbook, Gee & Co, looseleaf, 2 vols, £85.00 plus £60 (approx) per annum update, for 2 supplements). Volume 2 reproduces the IR Practice Notes and OPB Memoranda. Written by Robert Gaines, now with NM Financial Management.

David Wainman, *Pensions*, is a simple but expensive guide, oddly enough in competition with *Hoskings* from the same publishers. Gives the accountant's view of pensions, Sweet & Maxwell, September 1992, ISBN 0-421-45730-9, £55

Periodicals

Occupational Pensions, (monthly) Eclipse Group Ltd, ISSN 0952-231X, price on application

Tolley's Trust Law International (4 issues a year), Tolleys, £95

Pensions World is the trade paper, significantly improved in recent years, Tolley Publishing Company Ltd, 0181-686 9141, £65 per annum, cheap rates for NAPF members

Pensions Management, Financial Times Business Information, designed more for the broker market

PIRC Intelligence a sometimes idiosyncratic, though always sound, approach to pensions investment affairs, especially corporate governance, Pensions and Investment Research Consultants Ltd, Crusader House, 145/157 St John Street London EC1V 4QJ, ISSN 0924-234X, £795 per annum

Pensions Today, Monitor Press, 01787 467267, **www.monitorpress.co.uk**, cheaply printed, lively individual newsletter approach, £225 per annum, as is

The Pension Scheme Trustee, Monitor Press 01787 467267, which offers perhaps more information than most trustees need, £215 per annum

Benefits and Compensation International, Pension Publications Ltd, expensive but invaluable for international benefits managers, 0171-222 0288, £250 per annum

IDS Pensions Service, IDS, designed mostly for personnel managers, 0171-250 3434

IBIS, International Benefits Information Service, an amazing (and correspondingly costly) service

Governance, Gee Publishing, looks monthly at corporate governance, now the buzz-word for trustees, £150 per annum and

NED, Gee Publishing, looks monthly at non-executive directors for which the issues are somewhat similar for trustees, £150 per annum

IDS Pensions Bulletin (10 times a year), IDS, 0171-250 3434, specialising in company practice in pensions provision £138 per annum

Employee Benefits (editor, Peta Hodge), St Giles House, 50 Poland Street, London W1V 4AX, 0171-970 4000, has a slightly wider outlook than pure pensions £45 per annum

Weekly/fortnightly

European Pensions News, 01444 445520, covers every fortnight European developments, mostly on the investment side, £495 per annum. Sister paper to *Pensions Week*

Professional Pensions, MSM International, Thames House, 18 Park Street, London SE1 9ER, 0171-378 7131, £105 per annum. An independent pensions weekly.

Pensions Week, Maple House,149 Tottenham Court Road, London W19 9LL, 0171-896 2570, £84.60 per annum. One of the two standard pensions weeklies.

Investment and Pensions Europe (monthly) IPE International Publishers Ltd, 320 Great Guildford House, 30 Great Guildford Street, London SE1 OHS, 0171-261 0666, £135 or controlled circulation

Free from the consultants . . .

Bacon & Woodrow (Lisa Brooker) Parkside House, Ashley Road, Epsom, Surrey KT18 5BS, 01372 733795: Benefits Research Statistics (monthly);

Barnett Waddingham, 01753 890011 on request in writing to Senior Partner Adrian Waddingham

Buck Consultants, The International Financial Centre, Old Broad Street, London EC2N 1HQ, 0171-448 7000): Viewpoint (monthly)

Gissings, 0171-522 1561: Bulletins (every six weeks)

Hymans Robertson, 0171-831 9561: HR Perspective (quarterly), HR Review (quarterly), Quarterly Statistics, Glossary of Investment Management Terms, Investment Update (monthly), Investment Matters (quarterly)

Jardine Reeves Brown, 10 Albert Embankment, London SE1 7SP, 0171-587 0527: JRB Investment Quarterly, JRB Bulletin (quarterly), Investment Review (annual)

Lane Clark Peacock, 0171-439 2266: Briefing Notes (ad hoc); Briefing Plus (quarterly); Accounting for Pensions (annual)

Mercers, 0171-963 3224: Update (ad hoc), Review, (quarterly), Investment Consulting (quarterly)

Punter Southall, 0171-839 8600

Sedgwick Noble Lowndes, PO Box 144, Norfolk House, Wellesley Road, Croydon, Surrey CR9 3EB, 0181-686 2466: Trustee Briefing (around four times a year)

Watson Wyatt, 01737 241144: Pensions News (monthly) Benefits Briefing (ad hoc), Statistics

Personal pensions

A list of personal pension options is available in Janet Walford, *Personal Pensions 1998* Pearson Professional, 11th ed, ISBN 1 85533 483 92

Professor Richard Disney & Edward Whitehouse,*The Personal Pensions Stampede*, IFS, 1992, £20

An impenetrable package of statistics is published by the DSS, Analytical Services Division, *Personal Pension Statistics*, 1996/97, Government Statistical Service, 1998, £5.00

Policy

Mergers and acquisitions

The now deceased Occupational Pensions Board's report on what happens to pension funds on take-overs and mergers provides a good grounding on the provisions of what is now the Pension Schemes Act 1993 (the Ombudsman and all that): *Protecting Pensions*, Cm 573, February 1989, HMSO, ISBN 0-10-105732-6, £8.30

Demography

There is a huge literature on "whither pensions"; some of the more readable include:

Paul Johnson and others (ed), *Workers versus Pensions: Intergenerational Justice in an Ageing World*, Manchester University Press, 1989, ISBN 0-7190-3038-2, £22.50

If you want to know how pensioners feel, read the spoof of Christopher Meade, *The Thoughts of Pensioner Activist and Radical Granny Betty Spital*, Penguin, 1989, ISBN 0-14-012150-1, £3.99

Aging Populations: The Social Policy Implications, OECD, from HMSO, 1988, ISBN 92-64-13113-2, £12 pb, which is much shorter, 90pp – by 2040 the proportion of people over 65 will have doubled

Bryn Davies, *Locking the Stable Door, the Ownership and Control of Occupational Pension Funds*, Institute for Public Policy Research, ISBN 1-872452-51-5, for the left wing approach on what to do with surpluses, £5

Pension Provision Group ("The Ross Report"), *We all need Pensions — the Prospects for Pension Provision*, DSS, June 1998, Stationery Office, ISBN 0-11-762607-4 sets down the basic information need for planning the stakeholder pension. Lots of charts and common sense, £25

The pensions system

The background papers on the reform of the pension system in 1986 and later, are set out in what became known as The Fowler Report (in homage to the Beveridge report half-a-century before): *Reform of Social Security,* HMSO, 3 vols, Cmnd 9517,9518,9519, 1985, ISBN 0-10-195170-1, 0-10-195180-9, ISBN 0-10-195190-6, £3, £6,60 and £10, still a valuable source of material

Retirement

Allied Dunbar Retirement Planning Guide, Longmans, 1991, 4th ed, ISBN 990001995, £16.99

Guide to Living and Retiring Abroad, Daily Telegraph, Kogan Page, 1991, 5th ed, ISBN 749-404078, £8.99

Small self-administered schemes

Useful, short and sensible is John Hayward, *Administration of Small-Self Administered Pension Schemes*, which contains in addition all the working documents needed (the regulations, model rules etc),Tolleys, July 1994, 2nd ed, 260pp, ISBN 0-85459-879- 0, £34.95

Social security

Social security and its impact on pensions is a minefield.

The standard guide is Jim Mathewman, *Social Security and State Benefits,* annual, Tolleys, ISBN 0-85459 502-3, £24.95

State benefits

A very useful and understandable guide is *The Pensions Handbook 1997-98*, annual, Age Concern, £6.95

Legislation

The basic texts of the statutes and statutory instruments are published in a special series: *The Blue Volumes, Volume 5* (The Law Relating to Social Security: Occupational and Personal Pensions), HMSO, ISBN 0-11-761391-6, looseleaf, £22

Statistics

A useful guide, really designed for use by actuaries, is the *Pensions Pocketbook*, annual, NTC Publications 1998, ISBN 1-870562-78-X, £19.00

Monthly/quarterly

Watsons Statistics is a nicely produced monthly digest of pensions statistics, R Watson & Sons

Bacon & Woodrow produce a similar series every month

Aon produce a small list of statistics

Hymans Robertson, 0171-831 9561, produce a quarterly service which includes the figures that the others do, plus some intriguing investment statistics and graphs

The Government Actuary has published his Eighth Survey: *Occupational Pension Schemes 1987*, HMSO, 1991, ISBN 0-11-701225-4, £5.50 – which shows the speed at which the GAD works!

NAPF Annual Survey of Occupational Pension Schemes, £96.00

Pension Scheme Profiles 1993, an analysis of the benefits provided by 100 of the UK's largest pension schemes, Union Pension Services, £195

Directories

NAPF Yearbook 1998, NAPF, 0171-530 0585, ISBN 0-905796 50 0, £50.00

The principle directory is *Pension Funds and their Advisers*, AP Information Services, 0181-455 4550, 1998 ed £135

Local authority trustees (councillors and others) should have the *PIRC Local Authority Pension Fund Yearbook*, annual, PIRC, ISBN 0-904677-42-7, £115

Pendragon publishes Robin Ellison and Simon Freeman (eds) *People in Pensions*. It gives potted biographies of 1000 leading players in the pensions field; ideal if you are looking for someone to join your team, or are job-hunting (Pendragon Order department, Pendragon, Freepost, London NW3 1YR, 0800 289 5520, 1998/89 editon £75)

Investments

Pension Fund Indicators is published annually by PDFM (Phillips & Drew) and gives a survey of the various sectors with good graphs and charts (sometimes over-complicated). POA

Comparative surveys

The NAPF will run a search through its database, though you will not know the names of the other companies.

Japan

Japan Pension Funds Guide and Directory 1995-96, Asia Agenda International, 200pp with names and addresses of around 1600 pension funds, $1,000

Curuby & Co, *Japan's Pension Market to 2005*, ISI, Hong Kong, 852 2877 3417, 1998. If Japan is still in business, it has around $4,100B of assets in its pension funds, the second largest in the world. For investment managers. $299

Tax

Some of best guides are the simplest; recommended is Bacon & Woodrow, *Summary of Inland Revenue Limits*, free

The Pension Schemes Office *Practice Notes,* Inland Revenue, were published at the end of 1997; these notes are the bible of most practitioners and are also available on disk, £20

Also widely used by the practitioners is *The Legal and General Pensions Manual,* Taxbriefs looseleaf, plus updates, £28.00

Alec Ure, *Tolley's Taxation of Pension Benefits*, 1 March 1998, ISBN 1-86012 706, £85

VAT

Pension Funds and Value Added Tax, PRAG, 1989, £12.50, new edition expected in 1999

Trustees

A basic guide for trustees is: John Cunliffe, *The Role of the Pension Fund Trustee,* Croner, ISBN 1-85452-047-4, £12.95

Designed as a hands-on practical guide is Robin Ellison, *The Pension Trustee's Handbook,* Thorogood, 1997, 2nd ed, ISBN 1-85418-022-3, £25.00

Also popular is Roger Self, *The Pension Fund Trustee Handbook*, Tolley, 1992, 137pp, ISBN 0-85459-719-0, £15

You also need a free copy of the *Occupational Pensions Regulatory Authority's Pension Trust Principles: the OPRA Guide for Pension Trustees*, OPRA ,1997

Pensions on the web

If you want to avoid using solicitors altogether, try **www.lawrights.co.uk** – but there's not much about pensions. The most sophisticated and professional pensions service is Perspective (0171-393 7500) which contains the only fully hypertexted service updated daily on all pensions areas, and is really an intra-net rather than an inter-net service. It is designed for pensions professionals rather than intermittent users, and you need to be a subscriber. For other pensions information…

Official publications

Government publications are available at **www.national-publishing.co.uk** (a Stationery Office site); a similar route is **www.open.gov.uk/index**, which gets you into all the government sites. Press releases are slightly erratic; for example, some DSS releases are not on the DSS site but the COI site.

Forms relating to regulations are published at **floor.ccta.gov.uk:8080/dagii/welcome.nsf**.

DSS press releases and publications (only from the start of 1998) are available on **www.dss.gov.uk**; it also includes ministers' speeches, but some press releases fall into a black hole and may be printed but not issued.

EU pensions material is available on the DGXV website at **europa.eu.int/comm/dg15** (Monti Green paper, for example).

Financial services

The widest most appropriate site for financial advisers is **www.ifaonline.co.uk**, which although designed for independent financial advisers, contains information useful for all interested in the technical side of pensions.

Legislation

Acts of Parliament are on **www.hmso.gov.acts** and

statutory instruments on **www.hmso.gov.uk/stat**. That includes all public general Acts of Parliament from 1996 and summaries of Acts from 1987, and all local Acts from 1997. They are unamended. SIs appear two weeks after publication and are listed by number, but can be searched. Bills are available at **www.parliament.the-stationery-office.co.uk/pa/pabills**.

Debates in Parliament are available through the **www.parliament.uk** home page, and by clicking on the select committee site, it is possible to find for example the inquiry into pensions and divorce in the 1997-98 session, as well as relevant reports.

Law publishers

Sweet and Maxwell have a what's new page at **www.smlawpub.co.uk/whatsnew**.

Also available is the Law Society Gazette on **www.lawgazette.co.uk** and the Law Society on **www.lawsoc.org.uk**.

Law reports

All England Reporter is at **www.butterworths.co.uk/content/aller**, but is at a price: £3,000 to £7,500 per annum.

Casetrack is an expensive alerting and tracking service costing around £5,000 per annum which follows cases for every judgment listed; **www.smithbernal.com**.

The Court Service provides judgments from the Court of Appeal Civil and Criminal Division, Queen's Bench Division and Commercial Court and Chancery Division and Companies Court: **www.open.gov.uk/courts/court/cs_home.htm**. House of Lords decisions are at **www.parliament.the-stationery-office.co.uk/pa/ld199697/ldjudgment**. They are listed alphabetically since 1996. Employment tribunals will be available "soon". Some pensions cases can be found on **www.11-kbw.law.co.uk**

where the Chambers at 11 Kings Bench Walk have been involved! Australian cases are at **www.austlii.edu.au**, Canadian at **www.droit.montreal.ca/doc/csc-scc/en/index** (for Supreme Court judgments) and the United States on **lcweb.loc.gov/global/judiciary**. Court of Appeal decisions are available on **www.smithbernal.com**. The index to the Pensions Law Reports series is at **www.incomesdata.co.uk**.

Supreme Court decisions of the United States on ERISA are at **www.law.cornell.edu/topics/pensions** as is most of the US legislation.

For the United States generally, the finest site is **www.ebri.org** (Employee Benefit Research Institute). And it is useful to try **www.pionline.com** (the on-line service of Pensions and Investments, the main US periodical, which puts UK publications to shame. And it would be sensible to have a look at the distinguished work of the Pension Research Council at the University of Pennsylvania: **www.prc.wharton.upenn.edu/prc**.

Local authorities

A useful site with local authority pensions information is **http://dspace.dial.pipex.com/town/road/xoq83**.

International

A useful and comprehensive international site is **www.labournet.org.uk** and **www.unicc.org/ilo** for ILO materials.

Magazines

Magazine websites are usually frugal with their information; they prefer you to buy their hard copy. Useful company sites include, however:

- Pensions in Practice can be found as part of the IDS Pensions Bulletin at

www.incomesdata.co.uk

- Recruitment: jobs can be found on **www.msm.co.uk/profpens** which is the advertising section of Professional Pensions magazine
- Abstracts of general articles from Pensions Bulletin can be found at **www.incomesdata.co.uk**
- **www.monitorpress.co.uk** where there are details of Pensions Today, one of the better newsletters, and The Pension Scheme Trustee, which provides a little more than most trustees really need or wish to know.

Personal pensions

Details of personal pensions guidance can be found on the ABI site: **www.abi.org.uk**, as well as the regulators.

Professional and trade bodies

There is no shortage of press releases and technical information available from the trade and professional bodies:

The actuaries produce press releases galore on **www.aca.org.uk** (the Association of Consulting Actuaries) and **www.actuaries.org.uk** (for the Institute and Faculty of Actuaries). The National Association of Pension Funds has a tyro site on **NAPF.co.uk** and the Association of British Insurers on **www.abi.org.uk** again for press releases. Australian actuaries are on **www.actuaries.asn.au** and Canadian ones on **www.actuaries.ca**, both more useful than the UK sites.

Regulators

Financial Services Authority publishes some of its guidance on the internet: **www.sib.co.uk**.

OPRA

www.opra.gov.uk.

Academic

The Pensions Institute has odd abstracts of highly academic articles, mostly on economic aspects of pensions: **www.econ.bbk.ac.uk/pi**. In the United States, a vast publication programme is available on the website of the National Bureau of Economic Research: **gray.nber.org** including such classics as "The pay-as-you go pensions system as a fertility insurance" and "The value of children and immigrants in a pay-as-you go pension scheme". Many of the papers are in abstract form only, and full copies must be ordered and paid for ($5 a paper plus $10 for postage).

Links

You can find the way round may of these sites either through Pendragon, or through **www.irseclipse.co.uk** (which publishes Occupational Pensions).

Also highly useful is a sister company of Pendragon, which makes available astonishingly useful information already digested, from its own publications such as the Pensions Factbook (Gee Business Network **www.gee.co.uk**). There is a goldmine of pensions information and advice. It is not free.

A rather US-biased site is **www.financewise.com** which gives access to other academic and trade sites such as the actuarial institutes and IFS.

Technical information and odd snippets can be found on **www.watsonwyatt.com/uk**, organised by Watson Wyatt.

Addresses

Actuaries

The Association of Consulting Actuaries, 1 Wardrobe Place, London EC4V 5AH provides a useful list of consulting actuaries; handy for establishing SSASs.

The professional body is the Institute of Actuaries (in Scotland, the Faculty), but they do not generally deal with the public unless there is a complaint about an actuary's service.

The Government Actuaries Department is at 22 Kingsway, London WC2B 6LE, 0171-242 6828.

Advice

See Actuaries, Financial advisers

Compensation

Pensions Compensation Board, Room 501, 5th Floor, 11 Belgrave Road, London SW1V 1RB, 0171-828 9794 (fax 0171-931 7239) pays out where there is a deficit in an occupational scheme, there has been dishonesty and the employer cannot make good the deficit.

Disputes and complaints

Company schemes

Occupational Pensions Advisory Service, 11 Belgrave Road, London SW1V 1RB, 0171-233 8080.

Pensions Ombudsman, 11 Belgrave Road, London SW1V 1RB, 0171-834 9144.

Occupational Pensions Regulatory Authority, Invicta House, Trafalgar Place, Brighton, East Sussex BN1 4BY, 01273-627600 (fax 01273-627630).

Personal pensions

Personal Investment Authority, 1 Canada Square, Canary Wharf, London E14 5AZ, 0171-538 8860.

Personal Investment Authority Ombudsman, 1 Canada Square, Canary Wharf, London E14 5AZ, 0171-538 8860 (to be merged into one body with all the others called at the moment SuperSIB).

Insurance Ombudsman, 135 Park Street, London SE1 9EA, 0171-928 7600 can look at personal and group pensions operated by insurance companies, but you would probably be better off with the Pensions Ombudsman or PIA Ombudsmen.

Investment management

Investment Managers Regulatory Organisation, Lloyds Chambers, 1 Portsoken Street, London E1 8BT, 0171-390 5000 (to be merged into one body with all the others called the Financial Services Authority).

Financial advice

Personal Investment Authority, 1 Canada Square, Canary Wharf, London E14 5AZ, 0171-538 8860 (to be merged into one body with all the others called the Financial Services Authority).

Europe and international

The European Federation for Retirement Provision is an association of national association of pension funds (of which the NAPF for example is a member), EFRP, Hertogstraat 85 rue Ducale, B-1000 Brussel-Bruxelles, Belgium, 0032 2289 1414 (fax 0032 2289 1415).

Financial advice

A list of financial advisers in your area who charge fees rather than commission (qualified, but not necessarily recommended) is available from the Money Management Register of Fee Based

Advisers, Matrix Data Ltd, Freepost 22 (SW1565), London W1E 7EZ, provided you send them your address and postcode.

IFA Promotions can also give you three members in your area if you phone 0171-971 1177.

Lists are available from the Society of Financial Advisers, 20 Aldermanbury, London EC2V 7HY, 0171-417 4419, and

the Institute of Financial Planning, Whitefriars Centre, Lewins Mead, Bristol BS1 2NT, 0117-930 4434 but they are simply that; you cannot tell who is suitable for you.

Some chartered accountants provide financial advice (the Institute of Chartered Accountants in England and Wales, Moorgate Place, London EC2P 2BJ, 0171-920 8711 or in Scotland the Institute of Chartered Accountants in Scotland, 27 Queen Street, Edinburgh EH2 1LA, 0131-225 5673).

Solicitors are increasingly providing advice: The Law Society, 113 Chancery Lane, London WC2A 1PL, 0171-242 1222 (in Scotland the Law Society of Scotland, 26 Drumsheugh Gardens, Edinburgh EH3 7YR, 0131-226 7411) and especially the highly efficient Solicitors for Independent Financial Advice (SIFA) 01372-721172.

Investment management

The Association of Private Client Investment Managers and Stockbrokers, 112 Middlesex Street, London E1 7HY provides a list of members.

Solicitors operate the Association of Solicitor Investment Managers (ASIM), Chiddingstone Causeway, Tonbridge, Kent TN11 8JX, 01892-870065.

Legal advice

With all the free advice available from the internal dispute resolution arrangements, or from the

Occupational Pensions Advisory Service you should not normally need much legal advice; but if you do you are better off with a specialist pensions lawyer rather than a high street lawyer. You can get a list from the Association of Pension Lawyers.

Local Government

Local Government Pensions Unit, Department of the Environment, Ashdown House, 123 Victoria Street, London SW1E 6DE.

UK Steering Committee on Local Government Pensions, Layden House, 76-86 Turnmill Street, London EC1M 5QN 0171-296 6744 (Robert Gibbs).

Lost pensions

Pension Schemes Registry, PO Box 1NN, Newcastle upon Tyne NE99 1NN, 0191-225 6393 where you have changed jobs in the past or a former employer has been taken over, you may have money in pension schemes that you have lost touch with. The Registry may be able to help you trace the scheme so enable you to pursue your rights.

Policy

Department of Social Security, The Adelphi, 1-11 John Adam Street, London WC2N 2HT, 0171-962 8000.

Pressure groups

Help the Aged, St James Walk, Clerkenwell Green, London EC1R 0BE, 0171-253 0253.

Tax approvals

Pension Schemes Office (Inland Revenue), Yorke House, PO Box 62, Meadow Road, Nottingham NG2 1BG, 0115-974 1600.

Trade bodies

Association of Pensioneer Trustees, c/o Michael Norris, JB Financial Services, 18-20 Bank Street, Lutterworth, Leicestershire LE17 4AG, 01455-559711.

National Association of Pension Funds, 12-18 Grosvenor Gardens, London SW1W 0DH, 0171-730 0585.

Association of Pension Lawyers, c/o Jane Samsworth, 65 Holborn Viaduct, London EC1A 2DY, 0171-236 0066.

Society of Pension Consultants, St Batholomew House, 92 Fleet Street, London EC4Y 1DH.

Association of Corporate Trustees, Terry Williams, Bradstock House, 52/53 Russell Square, London WC1B 4HP, 0171-712 7500.

War pensions

The War Pensions Agency, Norcross, Blackpool FY4 3WP, 01253-858858.

About Eversheds

Eversheds is a single law firm with the combined resources and strength in depth to compare with any in the country, but made available through 18 locations in commercial centres in London, across the country and in Europe.

What sets us apart is our flexibility; the ability to deliver extensive, specialist resource when and where it is required, the ability to combine specific local expertise with the knowledge and experience of over 1,000 top-flight business lawyers and the reassurance that you are dealing with one of the world's largest law firms, but through an accessible and cost-effective local office.

On the following pages we give some basic facts about the firm which we hope will provide you with an overview of the support we can offer.

Eversheds at a glance

Eversheds is the largest law firm in the UK and has 324 partners and over 1,350 fee-earners.

The structure of Eversheds makes is possible to provide the full range of legal services through any of our offices, or on a national basis. To deliver this service, Eversheds operates specialist teams of lawyers covering over 30 areas of law and diverse industry sectors.

Eversheds' ethos is the local delivery of top quality legal services. Lawyers based in all of our offices share a comprehensive understanding of their local economy and business environment. They are also backed by the knowledge and experience of over 1,350 fee-earners throughout the whole firm.

The firm advises over 100 UK publicly quoted clients including some of the country's fastest growing companies. The November 1997 issue of the *Hambro Company Guide* lists Eversheds as one of the country's top four law firms in its league table of both stock market clients and fastest growing clients.

Eversheds' increasing investment in information technology, a rigorous quality assurance structure and ability as a leading firm to attract the highest quality staff, are key elements in delivering a quality service at a local level.

Eversheds has implemented quality human resource procedures; we have a rigorous selection process for trainees which has raised the quality of our recruits and we have increased investment in our solicitors' overall development.

Hambro Company Guide, November 1997

Fastest Growing Clients

RANK	FIRM	THIS EDITION %	LAST EDITION %	
1.	Nabarro Nathanson	16.3	22.3	(1)
2.	**Eversheds**	**12.0**	**16.1**	**(2)**
3.	Travers Smith Braithwaite	11.1	–	(–)
4.	Slaughter & May	10.9	16.1	(2)
5.	Clifford Chance	9.4	11.4	(4)

Hambro Company Guide, November 1997

Most Number of Stock Market Clients

RANK	FIRM	THIS EDITION %	LAST EDITION %	
1.	Slaughter & May	116.0	116.5	(1)
2.	Linklaters	97.0	97.5	(2)
3.	Ashurst Morris Crisp	93.0	94.5	(3)
4.	**Eversheds**	**82.0**	**92.0**	**(4)**

Eversheds pensions law services

Eversheds offers one of the most comprehensive pensions law services in the United Kingdom. Its team includes leaders in many of the specialist areas, including previously nationalised industries, and European issues, having been involved in many of the leading pensions cases. Eversheds is a firm recognised by the Occupational Pensions Regulatory Authority to offer prosecuting and trustee services. Specialist areas include:

Advice
- Scheme consolidation and mergers
- Compliance

Corporate
- Mergers and acquisitions
- Surpluses
- Insolvency

Dispute resolution
- Litigation
- Arbitration
- Pensions Ombudsman proceedings
- Mediation and alternative dispute resolution

Documention
- Deeds and rules
- Booklets
- Amendments
- Court applications
- Scheme merger and consolidation

European pensions practice
- Overseas schemes
- European Court proceedings

Product design
- Occupational schemes, including final salary and money purchase, COSR, COMP, COMB
- Unapproved schemes, including FURBS and UURBS
- Personal pensions, including GPPPs, appropriate schemes

Regulatory and compliance

- Inland Revenue approvals
- Occupational Pensions Regulatory Authority proceedings and compliance
- Contributions Agency negotiations, including contracting-out

Trusteeship

- Surpluses
- Merger of schemes
- Training
- Protection

Eversheds client base ranges from the largest employers and pension schemes, to individuals, and includes public sector schemes, privatised industry schemes, employers, trustees, members, trade unions, product providers, banks, insurers, unit trust managers, and governments and government departments.

As an Eversheds pensions law client...

As a client of Eversheds, I expect a full pensions law service. Set out below is the level and quality of service I think I am entitled to expect.

What I am entitled to

I am entitled to first class pensions law advice, helping me to protect and advance the interests of the business, the trustees, the officers and the members as appropriate.

How my lawyers should work with me

I need positive, practical and decisive advice.

I need them to develop solutions which are cost-effective, low risk and practical.

I need them to advise me and not equivocate.

I need user-friendly advice, not an academic treatise.

My team

I can choose my own team (including the partners) with whom I want to work; where appropriate I am entitled to an instant response and be able to contact my lawyers whatever the time of day or night.

I expect that responses whether written or oral will be direct and jargon-free. In particular, I expect you:

- to respond to all urgent faxes and telephone calls by return and otherwise within 24 hours
- to respond to all letters within a day
- on non-urgent matters to report to me at least weekly on progress (unless otherwise agreed)

- to ensure that there is always someone in your office from 8.30 am to 7.00 pm who is available to advise me
- to enable me to contact you outside office hours
- to talk to me before taking any action, including issuing or defending proceedings and incurring expenses such as counsel's fees.

Value

I expect a transparent fee structure with no hidden extras. I expect monthly billing and regular reporting on costs

My co-operation

In return I undertake my own co-operation, in particular:

- to tell you honestly whether a matter is urgent or not
- to be available if you need to take instructions or make decisions
- to tell you if I want something done differently, so that you can respond to my needs
- to pay your bills promptly.

The Eversheds National Pensions Team

The Eversheds National Pensions Team comprises some of the most distinguished pensions lawyers in the country, many of whom are regular speakers at conferences and seminars, involved in trade association affairs, and authors of the leading technical texts and training manuals.

London

Susan Andrews
Robin Ellison
John Hamilton
Richard Leigh
Harold Lewis
Roger Lewis
Kieron Mitchinson
David Wainman
Michael Wainwright

Birmingham

Ingrid Everson
Elizabeth Fallon
Lisa Gillespie

Cardiff

Ian Davies

Derby

Helen Miles
Giles Orton
Stephen Weblin

Leeds

Raymond Ainscoe
Helen Ball
Leigh Holmes
Katherine Livingston
Johanne Ratcliffe

Manchester

Gary Delderfield
Ronald Graham
Jacqui Timmins
Nicholas Walmsley

Newcastle

Kris Anderson
Patrick Dowdeswell
Susan Howe

Norwich

Ben Goodfellow
Robert Neal

Alphabetical List

Raymond Ainscoe *Leeds*

Raymond Ainscoe is head of the Leeds Pensions Unit. Educated at Bolton School and St Catherine's College Oxford where he was awarded a BA in 1975 and a BCL in 1977, he is a partner in the company department, having joined the firm in 1985. He is a member of the Association of Pension Lawyers and of the Pensions Management Institute, and spoke at the Association's Annual Conference on Equality and Retirement. He is a speaker for the National Association of Pension Funds, the Pensions Management Institute and the Society of Pensions Consultants, and contributes articles to Trust Law and Practice, Pensions World and Pensions Management magazines. He is a member of the Law Society's Committee of Management of the Solicitors' Staff Pension Fund.

Private interests include motorcycling (on which he has written several books), and classic Italian.

Kris Andersen *Newcastle*

Kris Andersen gained a degree at Newcastle University and was admitted in 1975. After working for Barclays Bank Trust Company for four years, he became a partner in Eversheds in 1980. He now advises employers, trustees and scheme members on all areas of non-contentious pensions law, including establishment and updating of schemes, the exercise of discretionary and fiduciary powers, appointment of advisers and Pensions Act 1995 compliance.

He is immediate past Chairman of the Northern Counties region of the National Association of Pension Funds, and has served on its Local Groups liaison committee. He has been involved in the development of trustee training programmes and presents seminars on a wide range of pensions subjects.

He is married with two children (both allegedly grown-up) and in his free time enjoys walking the hills with his camera, amateur dramatics and (plant) propagation.

Susan Andrews *London*

Susan Andrews initially qualified as a barrister and practised at the criminal bar. In 1986 she joined the legal department of what is now Sedgwick Noble Lowndes advising principally on occupational pension schemes. She also served on the professional conduct committee of the trustee company. In 1989 she joined Herbert Smith where she qualified as a solicitor and was admitted as an associate of the Pensions Management Institute becoming a Fellow in 1997.

She has acted for a number of household name PLCs, individuals and independent financial advisers on aspects of trusteeship, acquisitions and disposals, matrimonial, employment and insolvency issues, and on interpretation of scheme documents. She has also been involved in dispute resolution especially before the Pensions Ombudsman, OPAS and OPRA. Schemes advised have been the full range including final salary, money purchase, industry wide, personal, FURBS and UURBS. She is a regular speaker on the NAPF Practical Pensions training course, and speaks for the APL and at client seminars. She is a full member of the Association of Pension Lawyers and has written widely on pensions issues.

Helen Ball *Leeds*

Helen graduated in law with first class honours from Somerville College, Oxford, and obtained a Commendation in her Legal

Practice Course at the College of Law, York in 1996. She joined Eversheds on qualification to specialise in pensions law, having previously undertaken a broad range of drafting and advisory work.

Ian Davies *Cardiff*

Ian Davies qualified as a solicitor in 1984 after gaining an LLB from the University of Wales, Aberystwyth in 1981. He has been a partner in the Cardiff office of Eversheds since 1988. He advises on all aspects of establishing and running pensions scheme including documentation, multi-scheme mergers, ownership of surpluses, independent trusteeship and corporate aspects of mergers and acquisitions. He is the Pensions Team's specialist in small self-adminstered schemes, share option and ESOP arrangements. He is a member of the Association of Pension Lawyers, the Association of Pensioneer Trustees and he is also a committee member of his local NAPF. He writes regularly and lectures on pensions issues for various organisations, including, the IPM and the IOD as well as at seminars and training courses for Eversheds nationally. He is married with two children (twins). Leisure interests include travel, theatre and flying small aeroplanes from his local flying club.

Gary Delderfield *Manchester*

Gary Delderfield studied law and French at Keele University and worked in Bordeaux for a year as part of his degree. Having joined Norwich Union in 1994, he became part of their in-house legal team working on insured occupational pension schemes and in particular on the implementation of the Pensions Act 1995. He joined Eversheds Pensions Team based in Manchester in August 1997.

Gary is a member of the Chartered Insurance Institute, qualifying as an Associate. He is also a member of the

Manchester Group of the National Association of Pension Funds and of the North West Association of Pension Lawyers. Leisure interests include music, walking and playing rugby.

Patrick Dowdeswell *Newcastle*

Patrick Dowdeswell is head of the Newcastle/Teesside Pensions unit. Educated at Malvern College and Magdelene College, Cambridge where he was an Exhibitioner in Natural Sciences, he was awarded a BA in economics and law in 1971. He is involved in a broad spectrum of pensions work, including establishment of new schemes, transactional elements of pensions, advice to independent trustees and investment work. He is married with two increasingly worrying daughters and is a member of the Association of Pension Lawyers.

Robin Ellison *London*

Robin Ellison is National Head of Pensions. He was formerly Research Fellow in European Law at Wolfson College, Cambridge, and Managing Director of Finance For Housing Ltd. As well as being engaged in day-to-day legal practice, he is a trustee of a number of pension schemes.

He was the founding senior partner of Ellison Westhorp, a boutique solicitors firm engaged in pensions work only, which later merged with a national law firm.

He is the author of a number of works on pensions law, including a three-volume loose-leaf study, *Pensions Law and Practic*e, published by Sweet & Maxwell, and is editor of *Pensions Law Reports*. He has also published *Pensions and Divorce* (Pensions Management Institute, 1991) and The *Pension Trustees Handbook* (Thorogood, 2nd ed,1997). *Pensions Disputes* was published by Sweet & Maxwell in May

1995 and *Pensions: Europe and Equality* (2nd ed) in September 1995. He is a regular broadcaster, including frequent contributions to Moneybox (BBC Radio 4). He is the legal correspondent to *Pensions World*, the trade journal. Recent publications (1998) include *European Pensions Law* (Butterworths) *Family Breakdown and Pensions* (with Maggie Rae) (Butterworths), *The Pensions Pocket Book* (Simon & Schuster) and *The Pensions Practice* (Pendragon).

For some years he has been a member of the Council of the National Association of Pension Funds, the UK trade body, and a member of its Investment Committee. He was for eight years until its dissolution a member of the Occupational Pensions Board (the former UK supervisory authority) and is a member of the Confederation of British Industry (the employers' association) Pensions Panel. He is Vice President of the Double Century Club, the society for the study of EU life and pensions matters. In 1997 he was made the first solicitor Honorary Fellow of the Pensions Management Institute and was awarded the Wallace Prize for pensions literature.

Ingrid Everson *Birmingham*

Ingrid Everson is a senior associate in Eversheds Birmingham. After being awarded a 2.1 in law from Bristol University she was admitted as a solicitor in 1982. After completing articles with another large commercial practice in Birmingham, she joined Eversheds in Manchester in 1992 and returned to Birmingham in August 1993. Ingrid has experience of a broad range of pensions work including the pensions aspects of large sales and acquisitions.

In particular, she has dealt with the pensions aspects of various corporate sales and acquisitions including a recent £100 million acquisition which involved agreeing transfer arrangements between a number of final salary schemes and post-acquisition advice in connection with a scheme acquired with a substantial surplus and its possible merger with another scheme.

On secondment to Eversheds Pension Trustees Ltd she has acted in the trusteeship of an insolvent scheme with over 2,000 members, having the day-to-day control of administration, liaison with the scheme's professional advisers, preparation for trustees meetings, and progress towards final winding-up.

She had prepared interim and definitive documentation for a whole range of final salary and money purchase schemes, assisted on the pensions aspects of the restructuring of a public airport company, advised several groups of trustees and companies in connection with claims made in members' divorce proceedings in relation to their company schemes and advised on the structure of unfunded and funded arrangements for senior employees and directors and drafting appropriate UURB and FURB deeds.

In the contentious area, she has advised a major insurance company in proceedings issued for recovery of a substantial shortfall in an inaccurately calculated transfer sum and assisted a corporate trustee in proceedings issued by a member of an executive pension scheme alleging a shortfall in the lump sum and residual pension provided to him.

She is a member of the Association of Pension Lawyers and Solicitors Family Law Association and was a recent past Chairman of Solicitors Family Law Association (West Midlands Region). She sits as part-time Chairman of Child Support Appeal Tribunal.

Liz Fallon *Birmingham*

Liz Fallon is a partner and Head of Pensions, Eversheds Birmingham. Admitted as a solicitor in 1983 she took a degree in law and German at the University of Kent and has spent time at the Johannes Gutenberg University. She has advised on the establishment of a new scheme mirroring the benefit structure of the Local Government Pension Scheme, on the move into the private sector of a previously publicly-owned airport. She has co-ordinated the winding-up of five closed pension schemes with combined assets of £11 million, acted on behalf of both the trustees and the membership in a non-contentious application of surplus scheme assets by the trustees among the scheme members and the employing members. In mergers she handled a £94 million acquisition involving both UK and EU pension aspects and she regularly advises insolvency practitioners on pensions issues and on equal treatment matters. She advises on surpluses and executive severances and as a director of Eversheds Pension Trustees Ltd on independent trusteeship generally.

She writes regularly for *Pension Age, Finance Midlands and Employers' Law*, and lectures widely on pensions topics for Industrial Relations Services, Employers Engineering Federation and the Institute of Actuaries at their annual conference as well as training for OPRA.

Lisa Gillespie *Birmingham*

Lisa Gillespie is an associate in the Birmingham Pensions Group. She took an MA in modern and medieval languages and law at Newnham College, Cambridge, then after articles, she specialised in property law with another large commercial Birmingham practice for several years. Following a career break, Lisa joined Eversheds in 1990 to practice pensions law.

Her pensions expertise ranges widely; she has set up and prepared interim and definitive documentation for final salary schemes, contracted-out money purchase schemes, contracted-in money purchase schemes and hybrid final salary and money purchase schemes and in each case dealing with submissions to the Revenue and contracting-out notices as appropriate.

Working with Eversheds Pension Trustees Ltd, she has acted in the independent trusteeship and winding up of a large insolvent scheme.

Lisa has also advised a PLC on its proposals to merge its "works" and "staff" schemes, and given advice to various boards of trustees proposals to implement equalisation of pension benefits for men and women. She has advised on and effected the documentation necessary to change a scheme from final salary to money purchase, vetted definitive documentation produced by pensions consultants, and advised a Chairman and fellow Director on maximising their pension entitlement under their occupational pension scheme in the light of the earnings cap and their other pension entitlements.

She is a member of the Association of Pension Lawyers, the National Association of Pension Funds and the Midlands Life and Pensions Society.

Lisa is co-author of the *Maternity Manual* first published 1994 by CCH Editions. She speaks at internal and external seminars on issues in pensions. She is also a guest speaker at events organised by bodies such as the Institute of Personnel and Development and the Association of Pension Lawyers.

Ben Goodfellow *Norwich*

Ben Goodfellow read law at Cambridge and trained with Macfarlanes in London where he later became an assistant solicitor. He joined Eversheds in 1973, becoming a partner in 1976. In recent years he has concentrated on advising businesses on employee benefits, pensions and taxation matters including the establishment of share option and pension schemes, the review and updating of schemes, winding-up of schemes on cessation of trading and on mergers and acquisitions. Clients include Eastern Counties Newspapers, Tamaris plc, Nursing Home Properties plc, Bespak plc, Tom Hoskins plc and Startrite Shoes.

Ronald Graham *Manchester*

Ronald Graham obtained a degree in law from Oxford University and a post-graduate qualification from Cambridge. He qualified as a solicitor in 1985, becoming a partner in Eversheds in 1990. He is a committee member of the Manchester Group of the National Association of Pension Funds and a full member of the Association of Pension Lawyers. Having previously had a wide-ranging commercial law practice, he now specialises exclusively in pensions.

His recent work has included a broad range of pension matters: the establishment of new schemes, scheme mergers, advice to independent trustees and to employers and trustees of occupational schemes. He is a regular speaker at client seminars, and appears as a guest speaker in seminars for actuarial firms.

John Hamilton *London*

John Hamilton has an LLB degree in law from Birmingham University. He qualified in September 1997 and has worked with Guardian Royal Exchange's legal department on a variety of pensions, insurance and financial services issues before joining Eversheds.

Leigh Holmes *Leeds*

Leigh Holmes was admitted as a solicitor in 1994 after training in the Leeds office. She gained a law degree from Oxford University and took her professional training at Leeds Polytechnic. She works mostly on pensions aspects of corporate sales, acquisitions and MBOs. She is a student member of the Pensions Management Institute and is qualifying for the APMI, Treasurer of the North Eastern region of the Association of Pension Lawyers, an associate of the APLs national group and of the Yorkshire region of the National Association of Pension Funds.

Susan Howe *Newcastle*

Susan Howe gained an LLB at University College, London with first class honours, and was admitted as a solicitor in 1989, qualifying with Slaughter & May. As a litigator she is involved in pension arbitration and litigation, and compliance and regulatory work. She is a member of Network Northumbria.

Richard Leigh *London*

Richard Leigh is an associate with the London office, having joined them at the beginning of 1998. Before that he was with Bristol solicitors, Burges Salmon, a leading regional law firm.

After serving articles in Lincoln's Inn during the 1970s, he spent four years in London as a trust and property lawyer before moving West, first as a partner in a small high street practice, and then as an in-house lawyer for

Allied-Lyons (as it then was). During his ten years there, he became involved in pensions, and joined the Association of Pension Lawyers as a full member in 1985. In 1994 he returned to private practice as Head of Pensions at Bevan Ashford before joining Burges Salmon at the beginning of 1996.

He founded and has been Chairman of the Association of Pension Lawyers' Western Group, and is a member of the APLs Education and Seminars Committee. He is also a former Council Member of the NAPF.

He writes and lectures on pensions issues and enjoys music, food and sailing. He is married with two children.

Harold Lewis *London*

Harold Lewis is London Head of Pensions Litigation and Compliance. Having been brought up in Australia and obtained a degree from Sydney University, he moved to England where he obtained a BA in law with first class honours from Sussex University. He was admitted as a solicitor in 1980 and became a partner with Eversheds in 1985

Throughout his career, Harold has handled a wide variety of commercial disputes. These include shareholders, sale of goods, partnership, property, banking and insolvency disputes. In the construction and engineering fields, his experience includes acting for a German steel and heavy equipment manufacturer in relation to claims arising from the collapse of a very large state-of-the-art mobile crane.

He has worked with a number of foreign clients including Germans, Koreans, Russians, Arabs and Israelis. These experiences have helped him recognise the difficulties caused by cross-cultural sensitivities and misunderstandings.

Over the last three years, he has concentrated on dealing with pension disputes. He has dealt with many complaints to the Pensions Ombudsman and under the internal dispute resolution procedures established in accordance with the Pensions Act 1995. He has also acted for parties in High Court litigation involving transfer payments and the use of pension fund surpluses and for individuals whose activities as trustees and administrators are being investigated by the Occupational Pensions Regulatory Authority.

Roger Lewis *London*

Roger Lewis is a solicitor and partner in Eversheds; he is Head of the London Pensions Group. He qualified as a solicitor in 1978 and practised as a general corporate and commercial lawyer until the mid 1980s, since which time he has increasingly specialised in pensions law.

He presently advises a number of major pension schemes, including the Electricity Supply Pension Scheme, the industry-wide scheme for the electricity industry in England and Wales, and acted for that scheme and for the Railways Pension Scheme during the privatisation of their respective industries.

Roger graduated in 1966 from Balliol College, Oxford with a degree in physics and joined IBM as a systems analyst. In 1969 he moved to GEC where he was involved in a number of technical and managerial positions. In 1973 he took up a two-year post with the Commission of the European Communities in Brussels, before turning his attention to the law.

Roger is married with two children; his leisure activities include golf, tennis, music and the theatre.

Katherine Livingston *Leeds*

Katherine Livingston studied law at Leeds University. Articled with Eversheds, she joined the Commercial Litigation Department on qualifying in 1993. She is now a specialist in financial services, pensions litigation and dispute resolution, and a member of the Financial Business Unit.

Helen Miles *Derby*

Helen Miles is an associate in the Pensions Team of Eversheds East Midlands. She advises on a wide range of pensions issues with particular experience in the pensions aspects of mergers and acquisitions, scheme documentation and day-to-day advice for employers and trustees. She graduated from Nottingham University with an LLB and trained in Birmingham, being admitted in 1994. As well as her experience in giving legal advice to employers and trustees, she was company secretary of a pension trustee subsidiary of another law firm, where she became involved in trusteeship practice for both active schemes and schemes in wind-up. She works out of the Derby and Nottingham offices. She is a full member of the Association of Pension Lawyers and the East Midlands NAPF. Private interests include music and sport, playing the cornet and euphonium in brass bands, playing tennis and swimming.

Kieron Mitchinson *London*

Keiron Mitchinson has an honours degree in law from St Edmund Hall, Oxford. His traineeship included work in banking, litigation and then pensions. Qualifiyng in 1998, he remained with the Pensions Team.

Robert Neal *Norwich*

Robert Neal studied history at Cambridge University. He worked in the computer industry for nine years, the last four of them as manager of the time recording system of the London office at BDO Stoy Hayward. Joining Eversheds, he qualified as a solicitor in 1997, obtaining a distinction in the Legal Practice Course. He specialises in company tax and pensions.

Giles Orton *Derby*

Giles Orton is a partner and Head of the Litigation, Employment and Pensions Department of Eversheds East Midlands (Nottingham and Derby). His particular speciality is pension disputes and winding-up of schemes. He graduated from Queen's College, Oxford, joining Eversheds in 1987. He has appeared frequently in the press and broadcast media following involvement in a number of high-profile cases involving the pension funds of Imperial Tobacco, Mirror Group, Express Newspapers and Lloyds Bank. He is a full member of the Association of Pension Lawyers, and Chairman of its Pensions Litigation Committee. He is also a member of the East Midlands Committee of the National Association of Pension Funds. Married with three children, his interests include high church, sailing and country sports.

Johanne Ratcliffe *Leeds*

Johanne graduated in law with first class honours from Oxford Brookes University in 1995, having previously been employed in banking and financial services. As well as having over ten years' experience in the financial services sector, she has over two years' experience of pensions law in a commercial practice. Johanne joined the Pensions Team at the Leeds office of Eversheds in May 1998.

Jacqui Timmins *Manchester*

Jacqui Timmins studied law with French at Birmingham University and Limoges University. She was articled at Wragge & Co, a leading commercial law firm in the Midlands, and on qualifying in 1991 joined the pensions department. She joined Eversheds in 1995 where she concentrates on commercial aspects of pensions, especially in relation to industry-wide schemes.

She is a full member of the Association of Pension Lawyers and presents talks at both local and national APL courses. She is a member of the Manchester Group of the National Association of Pension Funds.

David Wainman *London*

David Wainman specialises in the taxation aspects of pension funds. He qualified as a chartered accountant in 1960 and for 20 years was tax partner in one of the big six accounting firms. A merger in 1989 enabled him to take "early retirement" and he joined Waltons & Morse, the insurance practice which later merged with Eversheds, advising on the accounting, tax and company law aspects of acquisitions and other transactions. He also advised on procedural and actuarial implications of the pension schemes involved and wrote a standard text *Pensions* published by Sweet and Maxwell in 1992.

He is a frequent contributor to *Tax Journa*l, and was for six years tax correspondent for the Financial Times. He has also written *Currency Fluctuation* (Woodhead Faulkner, 1984, 2nd ed), *Leasing* (Sweet & Maxwell, 1995, 2nd ed) and Company Structures (Sweet & Maxwell, 1995).

Michael Wainwright *London*

Michael Wainwright, a partner at Eversheds, specialises in personal pensions and pensions regulation and compliance. Previously a partner at Rowe & Maw he has worked for over 12 years on commercial and regulatory matters for clients in the financial services industry. More recently, he has advised on the merger of Hill Samuel Life and Abbey Life, the establishment of unit trusts and OEIC operations, offshore funds, unitisation of investment trusts, reporting on pensions mis-selling reviews, design of personal pension products, outsourcing and computer services agreements and regulatory investigations. He advises OPS members of IMRO on compliance matters, and drafts fund management agreements and custody agreements. He is a member of the committee of the Life Assurance Legal Society.

Nicholas Walmsley *Manchester*

Nicholas Walmsley is one of the country's leading experts on the regulation of financial service businesses and has acted for many prominent UK and international clients. He was singled out by The Legal 500, the client's guide to UK law firms which said that he was "deemed … to have encyclopedic knowledge of the law of fraud, money laundering and enforcement". He writes and speaks widely on regulation and compliance topics. His pensions practice includes advising on the pensions mis-selling review and on OPS IMRO schemes.

Stephen Weblin *Derby*

Stephen Weblin is a documentation specialist involved in drafting and trusteeship. He trained with United Kingdom Provident (UKPI) in the Salisbury head office and with Willis Faber in Birmingham, and has worked in pensions administration both for UKPI and Sedgwick Noble Lowndes. Drafting work includes the consolidation of complex documents, explanatory booklets and letters for special executive benefits, as well as discontinuances. He is an associate of the Chartered Institute of Insurance, and is a classic car owner.

Eversheds offices

London

Senator House
85 Queen Victoria Street
London EC4V 4JL
Tel: 0171-919 4500
Fax: 0171-919 4919

Birmingham

115 Colmore Row
Birmingham B3 3LX
Tel: 0121-233 2001
Fax: 0121-236 1583

Bristol

11-12 Queen Square
Bristol BS1 4NT
Tel: 0117-929 9555
Fax: 0117-929 2766

Cambridge

Daedalus House
Station Road
Cambridge CB1 2RE
Tel: 01223-355933
Fax: 01223-460266

Cardiff

Fitzalan House
Fitzalan Road
Cardiff CF2 1XZ
Tel: 01222-471147
Fax: 01222-464347

Derby

11 St James Court
Friar Gate
Derby DE1 1BT
Tel: 01332-360 992
Fax: 01332-371 469

Ipswich

Churchgates House
Cutler Street
Ipswich IP1 1UR
Tel: 01473-284428
Fax: 01473-233666

Leeds

Cloth Hall Court
Infirmary Street
Leeds LS1 2JB
Tel: 0113-243 0391
Fax: 0113-245 6188

Manchester

London Scottish House
24 Mount Street
Manchester M2 3DB
Tel: 0161-832 6666
Fax: 0161-832 5337

Newcastle

Sun Alliance House
35 Mosley Street
Newcastle upon Tyne
NE21 1XX
Tel: 0191-261 1661
Fax: 0191-261 8270

Norwich

Paston House
Princes Street
Norwich NR3 1BD
Tel: 01603-272727
Fax: 01603-272929

Nottingham

1 Royal Standard Place
Nottingham NG1 6FZ
Tel: 0115-950 7000
Fax: 0115-950 7111

Teeside

Permanent House
91 Albert Road
Middlesborough
TS1 2PA
Tel: 01642-247456
Fax: 01642-240446

and outside the United Kingdom...

Brussels

75 Avenue de
Cortenberg
B-1000 Brussels
Belgium
Tel: 00 322 737 9340
Fax: 00 322 737 9345

Copenhagen*

Advokataktieselska B
Eversheds
Ostergrade 27
Denmark
Tel: 00 45 3315 5033
Fax: 00 45 3315 5077

Monaco

Est-Ouest
24 Blvd Princesse
Charlotte
Monte Carlo 9800
Monaco
Tel: 00 377 9310 5510
Fax: 00 377 9310 5511

Moscow

UL Delegatskaya
3/B Moscow
Russia
Tel: 007 501 258 5058
Fax: 007 501 258 5060

Paris

42 Avenue du Président
Wilson
75116 Paris
France
Tel: 00 331 4434 7100
Fax: 00 331 4434 7111

Sofia*

Georgiev, Todorov &
Co
58-V Tzar Assen Street
1463 Sofia
Bulgaria
Tel: 00 359 2951 5665
Fax: 00 359 2951 8616
* *Associated office*